POPES
AND THE TALE OF THEIR NAMES

POPES
AND THE TALE OF THEIR NAMES

Anura Gurugé

authorHOUSE

1663 Liberty Drive, Suite 200
Bloomington, IN 47403
(800) 839-8640
www.authorhouse.com

Painting & photographic credits on page 140.

Copyright © 2008, Anura Gurugé.
All Rights Reserved.

No part of this book may be reproduced, stored in a retrieval system, or transmitted by any means without the written permission of the author.

First published by AuthorHouse July 8, 2008.

ISBN: 978-1434384409

Library of Congress Control Number: 2008906136

Printed in the United States of America
Bloomington, Indiana

This book is printed on acid-free paper.

FRONT COVER: *'Christ handing the keys to kingdom of heaven to St. Peter,'* a fresco painted, 1481-1483, on the walls of the Sistine Chapel by Pietro Perugino (1448-1523).

To
my youngest daughter
Teischan
whose name was inspired by that of a
great Renaissance-era painter of popes
and
to my son
Matthew
who attends a Catholic school
and whose name was inspired
by the 1970s group
"Matthews' Southern Comfort"

CONTENTS

PREAMBLE   ix

NOTES   xi

I BACKGROUND & CONTEXT   1

The Significant Facts   4

Name Changes Is Not A Given   5

Preserving St. Peter's Primacy   6

The Significance Of Name Change   13

Recurrence Of A Pope's Original Name   14

Regnal Names   15

The Term 'Pope' And Papal Titles   16

II THE HISTORY OF PAPAL NAMES   23

The Conventional History Of Papal Name Change   25

A More Critical History Of Papal Name Change   31

III TRENDS IN PAPAL NAMES   47

New Papal Names & Frequency Of Usage   53

The Ebb And Flow In The Popularity of 'John' As An Assumed Name   57

Trends In Papal Names By 250 Year Blocks   63

Trends In Papal Names By Century   65

IV THE NAMES 68
    Recurrence Factors, Durability And Popularity 73
    Reverence And Duration Of Reigns 78
    Why The Numbering Of The 'Johns' Do Not Add Up 82
    The Popes Named 'Sixtus' 85
    Possible Names For Future Popes 91

V RATIONALES FOR CHOOSING THE ASSUMED NAMES 94
    Multiple Rationales For Choosing An Assumed Name 97
    Regnal Names 109
    Papal Names In Common Secular Usage 110

APPENDIX A: MEANINGS OF THE NAMES 111

APPENDIX B: MASTER LIST OF POPES
          IN CHRONOLOGICAL ORDER 125

APPENDIX C: THE NAMES AT A GLANCE 135

PAINTING & PHOTOGRAPH CREDITS 140

SELECT REFERENCE 140

PARTIAL INDEX 141

PREAMBLE

"What's in a name?
That which we call a rose by any other name would smell as sweet."
– Shakespeare

"Sticks and stones will break my bones,
but names will never hurt me."
– English proverb

"... Names are everything. ..."
– Oscar Wilde

"The beginning of wisdom is to call things by their right names."
– Chinese proverb

The conclave to elect a new pope to succeed the iconic John Paul II convened on Monday, April 18, 2005. The devout, but in particular the cognoscenti, pondered as to which one of the supposed *papabile* cardinals would emerge as the latest Vicar of Christ. But an equal, if not greater number, many not even Catholics, were more intrigued as to the name by which the new pope wished to be known by. The chosen name would have significance: it would provide an immediate measure of the new pope's inclinations and intentions.

Papal names now possess a magic; they have become evocative. It is possible to wager real money on the name that will be assumed by a new pope. Prior to Benedict XVI's election in April 2005, some Internet-savvy folks were even registering potential domain names that might correspond to the new name. Suffice to say that a writer from Florida had purchased www.benedictXVI.com prior to the election.

Despite this inescapable interest in papal names, there has been very little dedicated analysis pertaining to their evolution. Consequently, there are inaccuracies and omissions. For a start, papal name change could be a much older practice than originally believed. This book is an attempt to rectify the lack of attention hitherto afforded to the story and the glory of papal names.

This book is a by-product of a larger, computer-aided papal history initiative I have been working on for the last few years – essentially as my latest hobby. Maintaining papal names, facts and figures in database form enabled me to sort and analyze data at whim – hence the detailed statistics and ranking provided throughout the book.

This book is not meant to be controversial, provocative or sensationalistic. The subject matter, though interesting, sometimes even beguiling, still does not, however, provide sufficient scope to incite *bona fide* dissension. Consequently, this book is meant to enlighten, and with luck, hopefully entertain. With it, I hope to put a stake in the ground vis-à-vis our understanding of the history of papal names to date. It should provide a solid starting point for others who wish to expand and elaborate on my initial work.

This book, in essence the outcome of a hobby, was by nature a one-man effort – with my wife, Deanna, Lynn Morin-Caron and Melissa Christensen doing the best they could to tidy up my English. During 30 years as a professional writer, I gained a hard-earned reputation for veracity. But I flirt with fallibility on a daily basis. Given that this is a brand new field for me and that I am opting to self-publish this book, there is a fairly good chance that there will be some unintended errors and oversights. I apologize for them in advance. If you see any of these, or want some clarification, please contact me at: anu@wownh.com. I hope to maintain two companion Web sites for this book at: www.popes-and-papacy.com and www.52904.authorworld.com. I will maintain an *errata* for this book on one or both of these sites.

I hope you find the information in this book of use and that you enjoy the story that I lay ahead of you. My motto, as it appears on my Web site www.guruge.com, is *"Think Free, Or Die."* In the spirit of that, if some of what is contained in this book gives you food for thought I will be delighted. Grace, and may peace be with you.

-- *Anura Gurugé*
Lakes Region, New Hampshire, U.S.A.
Spring 2008

NOTES

CR Number of recognized popes: For consistency with a number of online lists of popes, in particular the one found on Wikipedia, this book recognizes 266 popes – with Benedict XVI being the 266th pope. This number is one higher than what others use as their official number. This discrepancy exists due to the four day long papacy of the *original* Stephen II. This Stephen was acknowledged as a legitimate pope by the Vatican for 400 years – up until 1961. But he was then struck from the list because he had died prior to being consecrated as the Bishop of Rome. Older references still include him. There are also those who feel that he should be included given that he was an elected and acknowledged pope per the practices of his time. At the start of Appendix B there is an explanation as to how and why the current papal count can vary between 263 to 266 depending on how one treats Stephen II and the three terms of Benedict IX. The inclusion of Stephen II in this book should not cause any problems or misunderstandings since his inclusion is consistently stated throughout the book.

CR Sequence numbers: Sequence numbers, denoted by '#,' are extensively used throughout this book to provide easy identification of the popes: e.g., Pius IX (#256). The papal name lists in Appendix A and B both include these sequence numbers for quick reference. They also serve as a convenient index as to determine the relative orderings of the 266 popes. For example, when one sees John XIV (#137), John XV (#138) and John XVII (#141), it is easy to see that John XV immediately succeeded John XIV, while John XVII is separated from XV by two intervening popes. The start and end dates for all of the papacies are listed in Appendix B. Using sequence numbers is much less intrusive and cumbersome than identifying popes by their dates: e.g., Felix III (483-492).

- ❧ The context of the term 'name:' In most instances the terms 'name' and 'papal name,' as used in this book, refer to an elemental [i.e., basic or unqualified] name: e.g., 'John,' 'Sixtus,' 'Pius,' etc. Unless otherwise specified, or abundantly clear from its context, these terms, when applied to the 36 repeated papal names, do not refer to the qualified name [i.e., name plus ordinal] of a specific pope. So 'name' in general would mean 'John,' 'Sixtus,' 'Pius,' etc., rather than John XXIII, Sixtus II or Pius VI.

- ❧ Navigating this book: This book can be read, conventionally, chapter by chapter from start to finish. But it does not have to be. Each chapter and, in essence, each section is self-contained and can be read, comprehended and savored independently. Thus, it is indeed possible to use this book in 'lucky dip' mode. If read in this manner, the numerous lists and tables found throughout the book could serve as guideposts. There is also a select index that should help those who want to pursue a particular reference or theme.

- ❧ Abbreviations such as 'N,' 'SE,' etc. occurring in the context of geographic references, e.g., 'N Rome,' refer to compass directions. 'N' – north, 'E'– east, 'SE' – southeast, etc.

I:
BACKGROUND &
CONTEXT

he very first thing that a new pope must do, typically within seconds of accepting his election, is to declare the name by which he wishes to be known. He can retain his current name, use a variant of it [e.g., Marcellus for Marcello] or choose a new name. There are no rules, restrictions, guidelines or formulas that have to be heeded as to which option he chooses or what new name he may use.

When it comes to his name of choice, a pope, as with most other matters, has *carte blanche* authority that transcends earthly interference – even though it is not a subject that falls under papal infallibility. Albino Luciani demonstrated this, with panache, when he chose the name John Paul I (#264). This name contained three innovations, the most intriguing being that it was the first time a pope wished to be known during his lifetime as *'the first;'* i.e., the inclusion of the ordinal 'I.'

Prior to this, a pope using a hitherto unused name was not referred to as 'the first' during his lifetime. That would only happen later, posthumously, when a subsequent pope also elected to use that name to become 'the second;' i.e., II. What is noteworthy is that the cardinals who elected John Paul I, and had to announce his chosen name to the world, did not demur. The inclusion of the 'I' by Luciani was not treated as an unintended oversight. It was, instead, embraced and announced as a part of his official name. Elected heads of state and CEOs of large corporations can but yearn for such latitude.

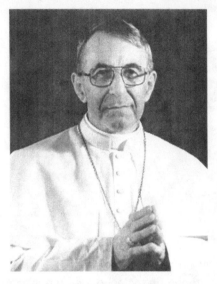

Figure 1: Albino Luciani, whose choice of 'John Paul I,' to honor his two predecessors, contained three innovations. 'John Paul' is also the first instance where a new papal name was used by successive popes.

This freedom to choose any name was also exercised by Marcellus II (#223) in 1555, albeit a tad incongruously. He is the last pope to date not to have assumed a totally new name. A noted Italian scholar, his birth name was Marcello Cervini degli Spannochi. Rather than assume a new name, he opted to use a minor variant of his existing name, i.e., Marcellus – the name of an early 4th century pope (#30). 'Marcellus' refers to Mars, the Roman god of war.

The irony here is that the first *documented* pope-elect to have changed his name was called Mercurius. 'Mercurius' was a reference to the Roman messenger god, Mercury – the one oft depicted with wings on his heels and helmet. Mercurius changed his name to John II (#56) to avoid introducing the name of a pagan god into the annals of papal names; St. John I (#53) having been a recent, much venerated martyr. This notwithstanding that the names of four other gods: viz. Dionysis (#25), the Greek god of wine; Anterus (#19), the god of requited love; Zephyrinus (#15), the West wind god; and Mars, were already a part of papal history.

So, the first papal name change was to avoid mention of Mercury. Conversely, the last pope not to change his name was called 'Mars.'

In Marcellus II's defense, however, it has to be noted that, in addition to the first Marcellus, variants of the name Mars had already been used by two other 4th century popes: viz. St. Marcellinus (#29) and St. Mark (#34). Mercurius, on the other hand, was without precedent.

These two incidents 1,022 years apart indicate the types of twists and turns that one can find when it comes to the 81 names used by the popes to date. Hence, this book.

In hindsight, Mercurius' noble goal of trying to avoid tainting the papacy with the name of a pagan god would appear to have backfired. The distinction of being the first documented instance of a papal name change has meant that Mercurius has become a well known and oft commented upon fixture in papal history – just as is the case here. Given his relatively short and uninspired pontificate, Mercurius is unlikely to have received this much attention if he had retained his original name.

The other firsts in 'John Paul I'

In addition to the preemptory 'I,' the other two novelties pertaining to 'John Paul I' are:

1. First instance of an assumed name that had not been the prior (or birth) name of a former pope.

2. First two-fold name.

'John Paul' is also the only instance, to date, where a new name to the papal rolls was immediately adopted by the succeeding pope; i.e., consecutive instances of I and II (#264 and #265).

Prior to this, there had always been at least two intervening popes separating the first use of a name from the next; the closest having been John I (#53) and John II (#56) – with 6 years and 7 months separating them -- and Pelagius I (#60) and Pelagius II (#63) – with 18 years and 5 months in between. Both of these took place in the 6th century, with John II having been the perspicacious Mercurius.

Sadly, both Marcellus II (#223) and John Paul I were to have very brief papacies, 22 and 33 days, respectively. Thus, their intrepidity in their choice of name figures large in their papal legacy.

Figure 2: Mercuris, the Roman messenger god, whose name was thought to be inappropriate for a 6th century pope, is depicted here by the Dutch painter Hendrik Goltzius (1558-1617).

THE SIGNIFICANT FACTS

- ☙ Number of popes to-date: 266 (per convention), including Benedict XVI (#266) who was elected in 2005, counting the short-lived original Stephen II (#92) and the three separate terms of Benedict IX (#146, #148 & #151). Refer to Appendix B.

- ☙ Total number of elemental (or basic) names used: 81.

- ☙ Elemental names occurring multiple times: 36.

- ☙ Names occurring only once: 45.

- ☙ Number of popes who retained their prior name: 139.

- ☙ Number of popes who assumed new names: 125 (counting Benedict IX but once, despite his three terms as pope).

- ☙ Most prevalent papal name: John, used 21 times.

- ☙ Name *assumed* most times: Clement, assumed 13 times.

- ☙ First name to recur: Sixtus; #7 and then #24.

- ☙ Oldest of the multiple use names: Clement (#4).

- ☙ Youngest of the multiple use names: John Paul (#264).

- ☙ First *documented* name change: John II (#56) in January 533.

- ☙ Last pope not to change his name: Marcellus II (#223) in April 1555.

- ☙ Longest unbroken succession, to date, of papal name changes: 72 popes, from pope #143, Sergius IV (31 July 1009) to #216, Pius II (elected: 22 September 1503) – spanning 494 years and 2 months.

- ☙ Current, unbroken succession of papal name changes: 43 popes, from pope #224, Paul IV (23 May 1555) to #266, Benedict XVI (ongoing) – spanning 453 years and counting.

- ☙ Most prevalent prior name: John (x14) and its variant, the Italian Giovanni (x16) – for a total of 30 popes whose prior name was derived from the Hebrew 'Johanan,' referring to the graciousness of God.

- ☙ Most popular papal name during the 20th century: Pius – 3 of 8 (37.5%).

- ଔ Most popular papal name during the 19th century: Pius – 3 of 6 (50%).

- ଔ First successive instance of the same name: Boniface III (#66) and St. Boniface IV (#67) in the early 7th century.

- ଔ First successive *assumption* of the same name: Pius IV (#225) and St. Pius V *(#226)* in the mid 16th century.

- ଔ Instances of successive usage: 13.

NAME CHANGE IS NOT A GIVEN

All 43 of the popes who have been elected since May 1555 have chosen, without exception, to assume a new name. Consequently, many believe that a name change must be an integral and inviolable ritual of a papal election. That the pope relinquishes his prior name and that smoke of some color emanates from a chimney above the Sistine Chapel have to be, overall, the two best known aspects associated with the pageantry surrounding the selection of a new pope.

Prior to the last papal election in April 2005, it was even possible to bet on what name the new pope would assume. Ireland's biggest bookmaker, Paddy Power (www.paddypower.com), had the prescience to have 'Benedict' as their favorite, at 3:1, ahead of 'John Paul' and 'Pius.' They also had Cardinal Joseph Ratzinger, who became Benedict XVI (#266), as their second favorite *papabile,* at 9:2, behind the 3:1 favorite Cardinal Francis Arinze of Nigeria. Arinze is now at 10:1 for the next election.

Paddy Power, however, had the name 'Peter,' at 8:1, as its fourth choice for a possible name. This was, at best, rather dissonant. 'Peter,' as described below, is probably the only earmarked name unlikely to be used by any new pope. Maybe this was but a tongue-in-cheek nod towards a supposed prophecy by a compatriot – viz. the 12th century Saint Malachy, the Bishop of Armagh. Per this prophecy, which is highly controversial and contested, the papacy of a pope named 'Peter the Roman' will result in the destruction of Rome!

The chances that the new pope may retain his prior name did not even figure in the top six – the sixth being 'Damian,' a hitherto unused name, at 80:1. Thus is the ingrained expectation that a new pope will always assume a new name. There were also those who were registering Web domain names, including a writer from Florida [U.S.A], who had bought www.benedictXVI.com well ahead of the election.

That name change has taken place, without fail, for 450 years should not be taken as a guarantee of its sacrosanctity. There was a 494 year unbroken stretch of name changes, involving 72 popes, that came to an end in November 1503 when Giuliano della Rovere elected to be Julius II (#217). Since Giuliano is a variant of Julius, it cannot be deemed a *bona fide* change of name. There have, however, been accusations that Julius, who earned the sobriquet 'warrior pope' for his ruthlessness and aggression, chose the name to denote his affinity with the great Julius Caesar.

Over the next 52 years, two other popes also opted to retain their birth names; i.e., the Dutch Adrian Florensz Dedal as Hadrian VI (#219) and Marcello Spannochi as Marcellus II (#223). Thus, 494 years of uniformity were punctuated by three exceptions within a relatively short time.

Since there are no covenants or even guidelines that dictate that a pope-elect must assume a new name, it is but the inertia of conformity and the momentum of tradition that continues to propagate this practice. The possibility, however, still exists that a future pope-elect may opt to retain his birth name, especially if it happens to be one such as Giovanni, Gregory, Nicholas, Paul or Alexander.

PRESERVING ST. PETER'S PRIMACY

St. Peter, the Apostle, whose original name was Simon bar Jonah, was the first to recognize Jesus as the Messiah at a gathering of Jesus' followers at Caesarea Philippi [Holy Land]. Thereafter, Jesus wanted Peter to take charge of running his church when his time on earth was at an end, as stated in Matthew 16:18-19: *" ... That thou art Peter, and upon this rock I will build my church; ... And I will give unto thee the keys of the kingdom of heaven: and whatsoever thou shalt bind on earth shall be bound in heaven ...."*

Christ's repeated requests to Peter to *"feed my sheep,"* (John 21:15-17), lend further credence that Christ indeed did entrust Peter with his flock. There is also Luke 22:32, where Jesus instructs Peter, referred to in this instance by his birth name of Simon, to *"strengthen thy brethren."*

Figure 3: St. Peter, the Apostle, the rock upon which the Church is built, is credited as being the first pope. Preserving the uniqueness of his name appears to be the only hard and fast tradition vis-à-vis papal name selection. St. Peter is depicted here with the keys to the kingdom of heaven in a 1473 painting by the Italian Franceso del Cossa (c. 1435 – c. 1477).

St. Peter is unequivocally revered by the Catholic church as having been the first Bishop of Rome and thus the first pope. This is the basis for the primacy enjoyed by the pope. Each pope, deemed to be a direct (i.e., immediate) heir of St. Peter thus inherits the mantle to nurture and guide the Church. It is, in essence, Apostolic authority via Apostolic succession – but in particular Petrine succession, where 'Petrine' pertains to the relationship with St. Peter. The crux here is the belief that the legitimacy and authority vested in the Church is based on the unique status, role and the subsequent mission of the Apostles – with Peter, the holder of the keys to the kingdom of heaven, being the Prince of the Apostles.

St. Peter therefore has a unique and sacrosanct standing as a pope. Consequently others elected to be his heir have shunned from appearing in any way to impinge upon his status. Thus, there has been a conscious effort among pope-elects to avoid reusing the name 'Peter.' So, to date, there has only been, one – and only one – pope named 'Peter.' Preserving the uniqueness of 'Peter' appears to be the only long-standing tradition when it comes to choosing a papal name.

St. Peter's presence in Rome (c. 60); his martyrdom (c. 67) at the hands of Emperor Nero's (54-68) Roman officials by being crucified, upside down; and his burial at what became the site of St. Peter's Basilica at the Vatican are by now accepted by most as a given. This despite the lack of any biblical or historical mention of Peter's activities in Rome.

The Peters who changed their name

Peter, or a variant [i.e., Pietro, Pierre and Pedro], appears to have been the birth name of 11 popes. All of them assumed a new name to avoid becoming Peter the Second.

The first known Peter to be *elected* pope was Pietro Canepanova in December 983. He had been the Bishop of Pavia [Italy], his hometown, since 966. He had also been the Holy Roman Emperor Otto II's (973-983) arch-chancellor to Italy. As with his father, Otto the Great (962-973), Otto II believed that the Holy Roman Emperor must have a say in the appointment of new popes. Following the death of Benedict VII (#136), who he had protected, Otto II unilaterally appointed Pietro Canepanova as pope, without an election. He was, however, Otto II's second choice; Maiolus, the Abbot of the Benedictine Abbey in Cluny [France], having been his first choice.

Pietro assumed the name John XIV (#137) thus preserving St. Peter's singularity.

Name change, however, was far from the norm at this juncture. There had only been three documented name changes prior to this:

  ℭ Mercurius/John II (#56, 533-535).

  ℭ Catelinus/John III (#61, 561-574).

  ℭ Octavian/John XII (#131, 955-964).

It is noteworthy that all of these first four name changes, spanning four and a half centuries, resulted in 'John.' In the case of John II, the impetus was most likely St. John I (#53) who had been hailed as a martyr just 10 years earlier. [Refer to the sidebar on page 9.] There is no record as to why the other two also chose to be 'John' – and there is even a possibility that Catelinus may have become a 'John' when he was made a subdeacon rather than when he was elected pope. Empathy with John I, however, remains the most likely scenario, but it is also possible that they may have wanted to honor John the Apostle or Baptist.

There is also a chance that Canepanova chose 'John' to curry favor with Otto II by signaling his intention to be like John XIII (#134), who predated him by a decade. John XIII, who had been beholden to Otto the Great, had crowned Otto II co-emperor on Christmas day 967 – though Otto II was but twelve years old. In April 972 John officiated at the marriage of Otto II to the then twelve year old Greek princess Theophanu, the niece

---

ST. JOHN I – THE 6 C. MARTYR

John I, an elderly deacon when elected, was the first pope to visit Constantinople, the Eastern capital of the Roman Empire. Dionysius Exiguus (*Dennis the Little*), a monk, while formulating a table of forthcoming Easter dates for this pope came up with the *Anno Domini* (AD) dating scheme. It obsoleted calendaring based on Emperor Diocletian's (284-305) reign; Diocletian been noted for his persecution of Christians. Theodoric, the then Arian King of Italy (493-526), was perturbed that John had not totally succeeded in convincing Eastern Emperor Justin I (518-527) to be more tolerant of Arians. Although there is no evidence that Theodoric harmed John I, the stress of the conflict with the King following his arduous trip to the East proved to be too much. He collapsed and died in Ravenna [Italy], Theodoric's capital. He was immediately hailed as a 'Victim for Christ' and his body brought back to Rome with much adulation. Hence the motivation to invoke his memory by propagating his name.

---

of the Eastern Roman Emperor John I Tzimisces (969-976) – a marriage that Otto the Great hoped would ease tensions between the East and West. John XIII had thus been a key figure in Otto II's life and Canepanova may have wanted to indicate that he would now assume that role.

Another Pietro, the Bishop of Albano [Italy], was elected pope twenty five years after Canepanova. The son of a Roman shoemaker, he had earned the unfortunate nickname *'Bucca Porci'* (pig's snout) that some, even today, assume to have been his real last name. His last name may have been 'Martino.' He chose to be Sergius IV (#143). ·

Sergius IV was the first pope to assume this name and the last pope of that name to date. He may have chosen it for its intrinsic Latin meaning 'servant of God.' It might also be that he wished to emulate St. Sergius I (#84), a forceful and competent pope who defiantly upheld Rome's primacy against interference from the Eastern Emperor Justinian II (685-695 & 705-711). Sergius II's (#103) three year pontificate was not particularly distinguished, while Sergius III (#120) was not noted for his piousness. He has been accused of ordering the murder of both pope Leo V (#119) and antipope Christopher (Sep 903 – Jan 904) as well as illegitimately fathering a future pope – viz. John XI (#126). So hopefully Sergius IV was not signaling an affinity with Sergius II or Sergius III.

The eleven 'Peters' who changed their names are as follows with 'John' being the only name chosen more than once:

#		Birth Name	Papal Name	Reign
1.	#137	Pietro Canepanova	John XIV	983 – 984
2.	#143	Pietro *'Bucca Porci'*	Sergius IV	1009 – 1012
3.	#186	Pierre de Tarentaise	Blessed Innocent V	1276 – 1276
4.	#188	Pedro Julião (Hispano)	John XXI	1276 – 1277
5.	#193	Pietro Angelerio (Pietro del Morrone)	St. Celestine V	1294 – 1294
6.	#199	Pierre Roger	Clement VI	1342 – 1352
7.	#202	Pierre Roger de Beaufort	Gregory XI	1370 – 1378
8.	#204	Pietro Tomacelli	Boniface IX	1389 – 1404
9.	#212	Pietro Barbo	Paul II	1464 – 1471
10.	#242	Pietro Vito Ottoboni	Alexander VIII	1689 – 1691
11.	#246	Pietro Francesco Orsini	Benedict XIII	1724 – 1730

Pietro Barbo, who became Paul II (#212) was the nephew of Pope Eugene IV (#208). He was made a cardinal deacon by his uncle in 1440 when he was but 23. Portrayed as vain, he is said to have *considered* assuming the name Formosus II because 'Formosus' is Latin for beautiful (or in this case handsome). This could have been a rather incongruous choice.

Formosus (#112), though astute, pious and caring, ran afoul of Rome's turbulent secular politics. Nine months after his death, his decomposing body was exhumed and subjected to an humiliating mock trial by Pope Stephen VI (VII) (#114). This unfortunate episode came to be known as the Cadaver Synod. 'Formosus' was thus not a good name to invoke; Paul II was a much better choice.

It is not clear whether Pietro himself decided against 'Formosus' or if he was dissuaded from using it by the nineteen cardinals who elected him. If the cardinals intervened after he was elected that would have been a first, and to date the only known instance when such an intervention had taken place. The standard reference works on papal history, however, use the word 'toyed' to describe Pietro's initial consideration; indicating that he must have changed his mind without outside interference.

This tradition whereby 'Peters' unfailingly change their name started well before the *'Prophecy of the Popes'* by St. Malachy (mentioned earlier) came to pass. The prophecy is believed to have been written c. 1139 during Malachy's visit to Rome. By then, Canepanova and *'Bucca Porci'* had already set a precedent.

The sensational reference to a pope named 'Peter the Roman,' furthermore, only occurs at the very end – as the last entry in the 112-phrase prophecy. Some claim that this last phrase was not a part of the original prophecy and was appended to it in the early 19th century. Consequently, it is safe to believe that the Malachy prophecy has no bearing as to why popes avoid assuming the name 'Peter.'

The two 'Peters' who were further honored

Of these eleven 'Peters,' one was canonized, viz. St. Celestine V, and another beatified, viz. Blessed Innocent V. St. Celestine, from humble farming stock, had become a Benedictine monk while still a teenager. Drawn to asceticism, he withdrew to a cave in Mount Morrone [Central Italy]; hence his latter name. In 1244, he founded an highly austere branch of the Benedictine order, since called the Celestines. The papacy was vacant for over two years following the death of Nicholas IV (#192). Pietro del Morrone, by now a renowned hermit, warned the Dean of the College of Cardinals of divine retribution if they dallied any longer. The Dean, elderly, ill and now perturbed, had Pietro elected by acclamation [i.e., verbal assent].

Pietro, thought to be close to 85 by then, was extremely reluctant to accept the honor. He abdicated after just 159 days in office. During that time he, however, promulgated two decrees: one reaffirming Gregory X's (#185) famous *Ubi periculum* to expedite the process of papal election; the other granting popes the right to abdicate, which he then promptly exercised. Possibly due to this latter decree, Celestine is still cited by many as the first pope to abdicate. That is certainly not the case. St. Pontian (#18), St. Silverius (#58) and John XVIII (#142) are all believed to have abdicated, while Benedict IX (#146, #148 & #151) certainly abdicated twice during his bizarre three terms in office. What Celestine did, given his history of obedience, was to legitimize papal abdication, so that he would not be perceived as violating an oath.

Celestine was succeeded by Boniface VIII (#194), who, as an expert in canon law, had assured Celestine that abdication was permissible. However, once pope, Boniface, fearing the possibility of a schism, would not let Celestine return to Mount Morrone as a hermit! Instead, he had him imprisoned where he died from an infection in May 1296. He was canonized in 1313, at the behest of Philip IV of France – mainly to discredit Boniface VIII who had displeased the King. Celestine is featured in a 1968 Italian novel *L'avventura di un povero cristiano* (Story of a Humble Christian) by Ignazio Silone and a 1990 play *Sunsets and Glories* by the British Peter Barnes. He was the last pope to use the name 'Celestine,' now unfortunately and unjustly tarnished by his abdication.

The French Innocent V and Celestine V were in office for roughly the same amount of time: 153 and 159 days, respectively. Innocent, scholarly, published and once known as *"the most famous doctor,"* was the first Dominican to be pope. During his fleeting pontificate he set about trying to reunite the Eastern Church with Rome. He, however, died of natural causes before there was to be any progress in this matter. He was in his early 50s. Leo XIII (#257) beatified him in 1898 on the strength of his piety, pacifism and scholarship.

St. Peter's Years
The pontificates of four of the 'Peters' lasted less than a year, while that of another was but 15 months long. Though Boniface IX (#204) and Clement VI (#199) compensated for this somewhat with their long pontificates, the average length for these eleven pontificates was 4 years, 8 months. That is well below the 7 year, 2 month average for all the popes, and nowhere close to the legendary 25 years attributed to St. Peter's reign in Rome.

In addition to his name, the supposed 25-year duration of St. Peter's pontificate, the so called *'Peter's Years,'* was also venerated. The belief was that no other pope would surpass this quarter century record. It is even said that in the 14th century the papal coronation oath included a phrase that the pope would not reach St. Peter's landmark. To be fair, in all those years, only Hadrian I (#96, 8th c.), with 23 years and 10 months in office, had come close. Thus, 'Peter's Years' appeared to be yet another auspicious adornment of papal mystique and panoply.

In June 1871, Blessed Pius IX (#256), to date the longest-serving pope, overtook St. Peter's tenure – ironically around the same time that the

Figure 4: Blessed Pius IX was the first pope to exceed St. Peter's legendary 25 year reign. He was beatified in September 2000 -- the beatification process having been started in 1907.

papacy had to relinquish the temporal powers it had enjoyed over the papal states since 754. Though outmaneuvered in temporal politics, Pius, whose reign lasted 31 years and 7 months, was vigorous and effective ecclesiastically. He dogmatically defined the Immaculate Conception and rejuvenated the Church in numerous countries. He also convened the First Vatican Council (1869-1870), which among other matters, ratified papal infallibility.

Then, as if to underscore the demise of a long-cherished tradition, Pius' successor, Leo XIII (#257), also surpassed the 25-year mark. Leo, known as the 'social pope,' lived to be 93 and holds the distinction of being the first pope to have his voice recorded as well as the first to be filmed. The only other pope, so far, to have exceeded 'Peter's Years' is John Paul II (#265) whose pontificate lasted 26 years and 5 months.

THE SIGNIFICANCE OF NAME CHANGE

A name change is meant to signify, emphatically, the new role in life that is being bestowed upon a pope-elect. It serves as a graphic demarcation between what was his prior life and the promise of what is to come.

The symbolism of changing one's name to signify the assumption of a new and elevated phase of life has both biblical and monarchical precedents. The two Apostles, Peter and Paul, so closely associated with the Church in Rome, now headed by the pope, are both known for having their names changed at the time that they underwent a change in status.

Upon meeting him for the first time, Jesus told Simon that he would henceforth be called *'kepha'* (rock/stone). 'Petrus' is the Greek rendering of the Aramaic 'kepha' – Aramaic being Jesus' native tongue. 'Simon' comes from the Hebrew 'to be heard' (or 'he who hears') and is sometimes extrapolated to mean 'obedient.'

St. Paul (diminutive), as stated in Acts 9, was originally called Saul ('prayed for' in Hebrew). After he had seen the 'light' on his way to Damascus [Syria], he starts using the name 'Paul,' possibly to denote his new-found humility. (Paul, for small, may have been his *original* name.)

In addition, in the Old Testament there is Abraham ('father of a multitude'), who was originally Abram; Israel ('prince of God'), who was Jacob, and Sarah (princess), who was Sarai.

When it comes to modern monarchs an example is that of the extremely popular George VI -- father of Elizabeth II and the King of the United Kingdom during WW II. Prior to ascending to the throne on the abdication of his older brother, he was Albert Frederick Arthur George Windsor.

RECURRENCE OF A POPE'S ORIGINAL NAME

Once a pope has been elected, the Dean of the College of Cardinals (the titular Bishop of Ostia [Italy]) asks him: *"Do you accept your canonical (i.e., lawful) election as Supreme Pontiff?"* The pope-elect has the right to decline. If he does accept, he at once becomes the pope: *Pontifex Maximus* (the Supreme Pontiff). The Dean then inquires as to what name he wishes to be known by. The name he then pronounces becomes his official name.

The pope's original name, however, does still get used, *formally*, one more time. That is during the *Habemus Papam* (we have a pope) announcement. The senior Cardinal Deacon makes this announcement. He introduces the new pope by the name by which he was formerly known and then announces the name by which he will be known in the future. If the pope assumed a new name, his prior name will cease to be used, thereafter, on an official basis. In private settings, however, relatives and close friends may still have the option of addressing the pope by whatever name they used to refer to him prior to his election.

There is an entrenched and fondly held belief -- albeit never validated by the Vatican -- that a pope's prior name is (or at least was) invoked during the ritual to confirm the demise of a pope. Per this belief, the *Camerlengo* (Chamberlain) of the Holy Roman Church, when tasked with ascertaining whether a pope truly has passed away, starts off by addressing the pope, thrice, by his prior name. The hope is that, if alive, the pope would somehow respond favorably to hearing a name that was once very familiar to him. To maximize the chance of the pope hearing his name, the *Camerlengo* is said to use a small, ceremonial silver hammer to lightly tap the pope's head each time he calls out his name. This silver hammer aspect, beloved by novelists, is open to debate and contradiction, given that the Vatican has refused to confirm that this practice ever existed.

In the case of John Paul II, who passed away on April 2, 2005, after a long period of illness, it is believed that his death was at least first determined more scientifically by a regular physician; who was more than likely his personal physician at the time, Dr. Renato Buzzonetti.

REGNAL NAMES

Regnal name (reign name) refers to the official name of the pope. It is always rendered in Latin – the official language of the Vatican and a language closely associated with the papacy from its very beginning. Thus, the regnal name of John Paul II (#265) is *Ioannes Paulus Secundus,* while that of Gregory XVI (#255) is *Gregorius Sextus Decimus* – where *secundus* and *sextus decimus* denote the respective ordinal numbers 2 and 16. Similarly, Benedict XVI (#266), the current pope, is *Benedictus Sextus Decimus.*

A pope's regnal name is independent of whether he retained his original name, chose a variant of it, or assumed a new name. The regnal name is but the Latinized version of the name by which he wished to be known when he became pope. The term 'regnal,' meaning 'reign,' is not specific to popes. Monarchs, too, can have regnal names. There is also the notion of 'regnal years.' These denote time periods, in years, calculated from the start of a specific reign.

For 50 of the 81 elemental papal names the regnal name is the same as that of the Anglicized 'popular' version. See page 109.

Figure 5: Statue of *Ioannes Paulus Secundus* (John Paul II) *in Krakow, Poland.*

THE TERM 'POPE' AND PAPAL TITLES

'Pope,' from the Greek *pappas* (and Latin *papa*), means father. It was originally used by children in ancient Greece. It conveyed affection and respect. The Romans co-opted it later to serve as a non-familial honorific.

Until the 3rd century, it was commonly used to refer to any priest or bishop in much the same way that today's priests are called 'father.' Even now, parish priests of the Orthodox Churches in Greece, Russia and Serbia are called 'pope' by the locals. In the West, starting in the 3rd century, its usage was restricted to senior clerics – usually bishops.

The Catholic pope and the Bishop of Rome, at a minimum for the last 1700 or so years, have been one and the same. The Bishop of Rome is the Catholic pope and that pope is always the Bishop of Rome. This is a fundamental, inviolable one-to-one relationship. The Bishop of Rome is the more historic and formal title. This bishopric, said to be founded by St. Peter, is the basis for the legitimacy, authority and primacy awarded to the pope, as the successor of St. Peter.

St. Peter, as an Apostle, may not have considered himself a bishop, let alone the pope. The consensus is that following St. Peter, Rome also did not have a monoepiscopal [i.e., headed by a single bishop] structure till c. 140. Instead, there was likely to have been multiple councils of elders presiding over various, communal, 'house' churches serving different immigrant or ethnic Christian groups in Rome. These elders were known as 'presbyters' which, in those days, was a term synonymous with bishop.

The history of its usage

St. Pius I (#10) is now considered by most to have been the first sole Bishop of Rome. Consequently, the eight 'popes' who separated St. Pius from St. Peter are likely to have been the most senior of the presbyters governing the Roman church at that time. Therefore, referring to these early presbyters as 'pope,' as is the custom, involves invoking some poetic license. The term 'pope' was not used by any of these as a specific title and would not be used as such for another two centuries.

St. Siricius (#38), elected in December 384, is credited with being the first to appropriate the title 'pope' in its current sense – albeit still not on an exclusive basis. He is also thought to be the first to lay claim to the *Pontifex Maximus* (Supreme Pontiff) title that had been relinquished just a few years earlier by the Emperor. [Discussed further in next subsection.] A forceful pope, committed to promoting papal primacy, Siricius introduced the concept of papal *decretals* [i.e., edicts in the manner of an emperor]. In 386, in one of his first *decretals,* he proclaimed that no bishop could be consecrated without Rome's knowledge or by just one consecrator. Furthermore, he claimed that he, as the pope, was St. Peter's heir, aware that per Roman law an heir inherits the legal status of his forerunner. It was a useful legal ploy to further the cause of papal primacy.

Siricius was followed by St. Anastasius I (#39) who had a relatively brief pontificate of 2 years. He was succeeded by St. Innocent I (#40). The widely-held belief that Innocent was Anastasius' son probably stems from a misinterpretation of St. Jerome's portrayal of what appears to be a spiritual 'father-son' relationship. [Jerome, a one time secretary to Pope St. Damasus I (#37), created the landmark Latin Vulgate bible.] *Liber Pontificalis (the seminal 'The Book of Popes' that came to be in the 3rd century)* states that Innocent's father was also named 'Innocentius,' thus giving credence to a spiritual – as opposed to a blood – kinship.

Innocent I, who proved to be one of the most dominant of the early Bishops of Rome, was even more unrelenting than Siricius on the issue of papal primacy. He corresponded widely with bishops in Gaul, Spain, Africa and Palestine. He provided them with guidance on church law via *decretals* but took to using an imperial *"we have decided"* style. He maintained that Roman church customs were to be the standard and promoted Rome's role as the Church's appellate court – even invoking Moses' role as the final arbitrator over ancient judges in order to rationalize the latter. Given this assertiveness, he is said to have earned the sobriquet *'the first pope'* during the Middle Ages. The significance here is that the term 'pope' was obviously gaining traction as an appellation for the Bishop of Rome by the middle of the 5th century.

The exclusivity the term 'pope' now enjoys at least within the Western (or Latin) Church came to be as of the 11th century when it was so mandated by another forceful and primacy-conscious pope, St. Gregory VII (#158). It was contained in his 1075 *Dictatus papae* (Pronouncements of the Pope) which specified 27 propositions pertaining to the rights of a pope; one of them stating: *'His title is unique in the world.'*

The use of the term 'pope' to also refer to an office – as opposed to just being an honorific title for the Bishop of Rome – appears to have happened even later.

The term 'pope' is still used by the (Greek) Orthodox Church of Alexandria, as well as the Coptic Orthodox Church, to refer to the heads of their respective churches – albeit in concert with the term Patriarch and a reference to Alexandria. The initial use of the term to refer to the head of the church in Alexandria (400 years prior to its current tripartite division) is believed to have occurred around the same time as it was beginning to gain ground in Rome, and possibly even slightly earlier.

The pope, as the Bishop of Rome, is now the supreme spiritual leader of the Catholic Church [consisting of the Roman Catholic Church and the Eastern Rite Catholic Churches] and the absolute sovereign – as of 1929 – of the independent state of the Vatican City.

The pope's role thus combines, somewhat synergistically, spiritual leadership as well as temporal rulership. This duality has been true during most of papal history. However, the exact scope of the temporal rulership was subject to considerable ebb and flow, over the centuries, prior the Lateran Treaty of 1929 which created the Vatican City State.

The pope's official titles
As of March 2006, the pope has eight formal titles:
  i.   Bishop of Rome *(Episcopus Romanus)*,
  ii. Vicar of [Jesus] Christ *(Vicarius Christi)*,
  iii. Successor of St. Peter, Prince of the Apostles
       (previously Vicar of Peter),
  iv. Supreme Pontiff of the Universal Church *(Pontifex Maximus)*,
  v.   Primate of Italy,
  vi. Archbishop and Metropolitan of the Roman Province,
  vii. Sovereign of Vatican City State, and
  viii. Servant of the Servants of God *(Servus Servorum Dei)*.

The term 'pope' is thus informal, albeit still honorific, with the historic and authoritative 'Bishop of Rome' being the preeminent of the titles. In some instances, all the formal titles currently in use are appended together and used as a single, solemn appellation. Some consider this compound title to be the official title of the pope.

In 2006, the designation 'Patriarch of the West,' which had been a component of the full list of titles since the mid 7th century, was retracted, forthwith, without any prior notice. The Vatican stated that this designation no longer reflected historic or theological reality and was getting in the way of furthering unity among the various Christian churches [i.e., ecumenism]. 'Patriarch of Rome' and 'Latin Patriarch' are considered to be alternate forms of 'Patriarch of the West.'

Pope Gelasius I (#49), another strident champion of papal primacy, is credited with the introduction and use of the title 'Vicar of Jesus Christ'– where 'vicar' from the Latin *vicarius* means substitute. [The term 'vicarious' also comes from the same root.] Prior to that, 'Vicar of (St.) Peter' (Vicarius Petri), 'Vicar of the Prince of the Apostles' and 'Vicar of the Apostolic See' had been used by the earlier Bishops of Rome.

The Latin *Pontifex Maximus* (Supreme Pontiff), with *pontifex* implying bridge (or road) builder (between the divine and the mortals), predates popes and even Christianity by quite a few centuries. It was originally used to denote the head of the Ancient Roman religious practices. Around 12 BC it was appropriated by Emperor Augustus [commemorated by the month August] to apply only to the Roman emperor. This was the case until 382, when Emperor Gratian, the Western Emperor of the now Christian empire, relinquished the title, given its pagan roots.

Two years later, it appears to have been appropriated by Pope Siricius (#38), who is also credited as being the first Bishop of Rome to lay claim to the title 'pope,' albeit on a non-exclusive basis. But *Pontifex Maximus* was not as yet restricted just for use by the 'pope.' Around the start of the 5th century, it appears to have been used to designate the bishops of the various capital cities of the Roman provinces [i.e., the so called metropolitan bishops] with other bishops being referred to as just Pontiff. It is believed to have taken another six centuries before its use was restricted just to the Bishop of Rome – and even then without the 'of the Universal Church' designation, which came still later. The metropolitan reference now found in the official title, however, came to be in 1929, via another route discussed below.

'P.M.' or 'Pont. Max.' are often appended to a pope's name, particularly in inscriptions, to designate his standing as *Pontifex Maximus*.

'Servant of the Servants of God' was a favored phrase of Pope Gregory the Great (#64), possibly even before he became the pope. It was famously used by him, c. 596, in the letters related to St. Augustine's historic trip to England. It was, however, not universally adopted by his successors over the next couple of centuries. Some used it; others did not -- possibly taking exception to its innate humility.

Popes started using it on a regular basis during the 9th century, though not as a title that was their exclusive prerogative. That only appears to have happened in the 12th or 13th century. Even then, it might not have been a standard component of the accepted repertoire of official papal titles on a regular and consistent basis. It was, however, routinely used in the papal decrees issued at both the First Vatican Council [1869-1870] and the Second [1962-1965]. This was apropos, since overall conciliation was a major theme of both these Councils. Possibly, thanks to the momentum gained from its use in the Second Council, Pope Paul VI (#263) added it to the list of official titles in 1969, while at the same time retracting the phrase 'gloriously reigning' from that list.

Compared to the other designations, 'Primate of Italy,' 'Archbishop and Metropolitan of the Roman Province,' and 'Sovereign of Vatican City State,' are relatively new appellations. They came to be, collectively, in 1929, as a result of the landmark Lateran Treaty. This Treaty is also called the Lateran Pacts of 1929. It was a set of three agreements, containing a total of 75 articles, with the Treaty of Conciliation being one of the three agreements.

The Lateran Treaty finally resolved the so called 'Roman Question' that had surfaced in 1870. This had to do with the Papal States, with Rome as the final bastion, being unilaterally incorporated into the then nascent kingdom of Italy, to the chagrin of the papacy. The treaty, in addition to dealing with financial compensation, created the state of Vatican City and ensured that the pope had total and independent sovereignty of that state -- with supreme executive, legislative, and judicial power.

The Lateran Treaty was revised in 1984. The 1929 treaty was signed by Benito Mussolini, of World War II repute, on behalf of King Victor Emmanuel III in his then capacity of Prime Minister. The then reigning pope, Pope Pius XI (#260), was represented by his Papal Secretary of State Pietro Cardinal Gasparri.

Other papal titles

The most frequently used of the informal appellations are 'His Holiness The Pope' and 'Holy Father.' Variations, such as 'Most Holy Father' (*Sanctissimus Pater*), 'Our Most Holy Lord' (*Sanctissimus Dominus Noster*), 'His Holiness' (*Sanctitas Sua*), 'Most Holy' (*Sanctissimus), *'Most

Blessed Father' (*Beatissimus Pater*), 'His Beatitude' (*Beatitude Sue*) and 'Our Most Holy Lord' (*Sanctissimus Dominus Noster*) are also not uncommon.

'Highest Pontiff' (*Summus Pontifex*), a variant of the *Pontifex Maximus*, is also sometimes used. Canon law refers to the pope as *Romanus Pontifex* (Roman Pontiff), thus indirectly invoking the pope's inviolable Bishop of Rome credentials.

In medieval times, 'Apostolic Lord' (*Dominus Apostolicus*) or just plain 'The Apostolic' (*Apostolicus*) were also employed.

One addresses the pope, in person, as 'Your Holiness' (*Sanctitas Vestra*), 'Most Blessed Father' (*Beatissime Pater*) or 'Holy Father' (*Santissimo Padre*).

Form and format of papal signatures

A pope uses two different signature styles depending on the nature of the document being signed. The most solemn and formal of papal documents are known as 'bulls,' where the name comes from the metal seal that used to be attached to such documents. In rare instances, this seal might even be made out of gold. The term 'bull' comes from the Latin *bulla* for stud, boss, or ornament; which in turn may have been influenced by the Latin *bullire,* to boil, referring to the bubble-like shape of such ornaments. Other papal documents, including encyclicals [i.e., a papal letter to bishops, a country, or the whole Catholic Church] are referred to as 'briefs.'

The signature used on papal bulls would be the pope's regnal name (without the numeric ordinal), followed by *Episcopus Ecclesiae Catholicae* (Bishop of the Catholic Church). Bulls, in addition, would also begin with the pope's regnal name prior to the title *Episcopus, Servus Servorum Dei* (Bishop, Servant of the Servants of God). The pope's name and this title at the head of the bull, along with a few words in Latin to categorize the nature of that bull, would all appear on one line, formed with extra tall, elaborate and elongated letters.

The metal 'bull' (seal) is attached to the document via strings of hemp or silk threads. One side of the seal would pay homage to the two Apostles who are credited with founding the Roman church – viz. St. Paul and St. Peter. They are identified by the contraction SPA SPE standing for <u>S</u>anctus <u>PA</u>ulus and <u>S</u>anctus <u>PE</u>trus. Note that this is one of the few instances where St. Paul's well-chronicled role in founding the Roman church is acknowledged. It is also interesting that, in this instance, St. Paul is mentioned ahead of St. Peter.

The other side of the bull would contain the name of the pope issuing the bull in the form: 'regnal name PP ordinal' (where sometimes the PP was spelt out as *papa*), e.g., Eugenius PP III and Leo Papa X. Since the late 1700s, the attachment of metal seals to bulls has been limited to those considered to be exceptionally important, such as John XXIII's (#262) bull to convene the watershed Vatican Council II of 1962. If a seal is not attached a red ink stamp is used in its place. As with the metal bull, the stamp invokes St. Paul and St. Peter with the issuing pope's name written around it.

Signatures on briefs are of the form 'regnal name PP. ordinal,' where PP. is interpreted either as *Papa* (Latin for 'pope') or *Pater Patrum* (Father of Fathers). Thus Benedict XVI's (#266) signature on a brief would be '*Benedictus PP. XVI,*' while that of John Paul II's (#265) was '*Ioannes Paulus PP. II.*'

Transcripts of the encyclicals of recent popes can be readily found at the Vatican website at: www.vatican.va.

Figure 6: A papal coin issued during the time of Pope Urban VIII (#236), showing Saints Peter and Paul on one side and Urban's Barberini coat of arms with its three bees on the other. Such coins served as currency within the papal states.

II:
THE HISTORY OF
PAPAL NAMES

aint Irenaeus, the Bishop of Lyon [France] c. 178, was one of the earliest of the defining writers on Christian theology. He had visited Rome, prior to becoming a bishop, to meet with Pope Eleutherius (#13) to brief him on the spread of heresies in southern Gaul. Between c. 175 and c. 185 he wrote a groundbreaking five volume treatise on the prevailing state of Christianity that is now referred to as *Adversus Haereses* (Against Heresies).

In the third volume, he sets out to refute heretics by arguing that various churches had maintained a perpetual succession of (orthodoxy representing) bishops. As a part of this argument, in Chapter 3, Paragraph 3, he enumerates the first 12 Bishops of Rome – this being the earliest acknowledged list of the founding 'popes.'

Irenaeus' list states: *"...To this Clement there succeeded Evaristus. Alexander followed Evaristus; then, sixth from the apostles, Sixtus was appointed; ..."*

'Sixtus,' considered a variant of '*Sextus*,' along with '*Sesto*' and '*Sixto*,' is a Latin word denoting 6th. It was thus a popular choice of name for a 6th child, albeit not limited exclusively for just that scenario.

The sixth 'pope' to succeed St. Peter thus happens to be called 'the 6th.' This would appear to be rather propitious, to say the least. Irenaeus, though, appears to have been indifferent to its remarkability. Maybe he knew that it was meant to be as such. To make it even more intriguing, many respected sources, for example, the 1917 *'Catholic Encyclopedia'* (now online at www.newadvent.org), and the *'Oxford Dictionary of Popes,'* note that 'Xystus' is the correct (or older) spelling for 'Sixtus.' The 1917 *'Catholic Encyclopedia'* goes on to even say that the spelling 'Xystus' was used to refer to the first three popes now known as Sixtus I (#7), Sixtus II (#24) and Sixtus III (44).

Nonetheless, there is little or no discourse, speculative or otherwise, that the 6th pope to succeed St. Peter may have had a different birth name than that by which he is now known. This Sixtus/Xystus incongruity is explored on page 34. All five of the popes named Sixtus are discussed in chapter IV against the background of a poem written in 1834 by Giuseppe Gioacchino Belli's that ends with the rebuke: *"Because not too soon another pope may have the whim of naming himself Sixtus the Sixth."* To make it worse, the conciliatory Sixtus III, who is believed to have founded the first Roman monastery, is still maligned as the Antichrist because his name as '6th III' invokes the dreaded '666.'

The blameless Bishop of Rome
In Titus 1:6-7, St. Paul, talking about those who should be made bishops states: *"...If any be blameless, the husband of one wife, ... For a bishop must be blameless, as the steward of God; ...."*

Given this emphasis placed on blamelessness, it again seems rather opportune that the

Figure 7: Pope Sixtus IV (#213) whose rejuvenation of Rome included the building of the Sistine Chapel – with 'Sistine' being a reference to his name. Michelangelo's ceiling, which immortalized this chapel, was commissioned by Sixtus' nephew, Julius II (#217) the 'warrior pope,' the 3rd but last pope to retain his birth name; viz. 'Giulinao.'

Le Pape Sixte IV

second Bishop of Rome after St. Peter happens to be named Anacletus (#3) – a Greek adjective meaning blameless and as such often associated with former slaves.

This coincidence, as with Sixtus I, is rarely, if ever, noted in the context of a conceivable papal name change. However, in earlier times, the very existence of this 'pope' was questioned due to the propagandistic nature of his name. In reality, the root cause of this confusion as to his existence was more likely a result of him being referred to as 'Cletus' in some 4th century documents – in particular in the list of martyrs celebrated at Mass.

In an era where information dissemination was slow and cumbersome, people came to believe that there had been two different popes, one Greek, the other Roman, called 'Anacletus' and 'Cletus.' 'Cletus' is now considered to be a shortened form of 'Anacletus,' probably influenced by this papal association. However, 'Cletus,' another Greek term, denotes 'summoned' (and as such also 'invoked') and possibly even 'illustrious.' Thus, one could speculate that 'Cletus,' a noble name in its own right, may have been used by early historians to circumvent the 'blameless' and 'former slave' connotations. Or maybe 'Cletus' was his birth name!

Again, as with Sixtus I, it is unlikely that any new documentation will be located, anytime soon, that could shed further light as to the exact birth name of the 3rd 'pope.' All that can be safely surmised, as some papal scholars have believed for a while, is that there may have been undocumented name changes prior to January 533 when Mercurius chose to be John II (#56). To this end, it should also be noted that significant amounts of church documents were likely to have been lost or destroyed during the bouts of Christian persecution that lasted up to the 4th century. This would have been particularly true during the campaigns by Emperors Diocletian (299-305), Valerian I (257-260) and Trajan (112-117).

THE CONVENTIONAL HISTORY OF PAPAL NAME CHANGE

Papal names and papal name changes do not appear to have received too much scrutiny over the years. Given the depth, breadth and aura of a pope's role and influence, the name by which he was known by does seem to be somewhat incidental and peripheral. Consequently, most accounts of papal name trends and changes tend to present a rather sketchy, superficial picture. The possible sketchiness, however, is never mentioned and there are rarely any caveats. That this has led to serious errors in some of the online accounts of the popes should not come as a surprise.

The conventional, sans caveat, history of papal name change is as follows:

ଔ John II (#56): The first pope to change his name was Mercurius. When elected in January 533, he opted to be known as John II to avoid having the name of a pagan god, viz. Mercury, associated with the papacy. He chose 'John' to pay homage to the recently martyred John I (#53).

ଔ John III (#61) : 28 years and four popes later, Catelinus, a subdeacon of aristocratic stock, becomes John III.

ଔ John XII (#131) : 394 years and 69 popes later, Octavian, the illegitimate son of Alberic II, the ruler of Rome (932-954), was elected pope pursuant to his father's deathbed coercion. He assumed the name John XII. John XI (#126) was his step-uncle.

ଔ John XIV (#137) : In December 983, 28 years and five popes later, Pietro Canepanova, Bishop of Pavia [Italy], was appointed pope, by the Holy Roman Emperor Otto II (973-983) without an election. Pietro chose to be John XIV to avoid becoming 'Peter II' [p. 8].

His appointment by fiat deprived John of Roman support. His papacy was contingent on continued Imperial backing. But, sadly, Otto was to die of malaria, in the pope's arms, less than a fortnight after John's consecration at the Lateran Bascilica – the official seat of the Bishop of Rome. Boniface (VII), was an antipope who had invalidly ousted Benedict VI (#135) in June 974. He was, however, forced to flee to Constantinople a few months later. With Otto's death, he again saw an opportunity to enter the fray in Rome.

In April 984, with help from the then rampant Crescentii family, Boniface had John seized, brutalized and deposed. John ended up as a prisoner within the formidable Castel Sant'Angelo [p. 27]. He died four months later due to starvation, poisoning or a combination of both. Boniface was also to die, unexpectedly, 11 months later – though the claims that he was done in by his own entourage cannot be substantiated.

Figure 8: Castel Sant'Angelo, on the banks of the Tiber, close to the Vatican Hill, which was originally built as a family mausoleum for Emperor Hadrian [117-138], but has also served as both a refuge and a prison for popes. John XIV (#137), the 4th known pope to change his name and the first of the 'Peters' to have changed his name to avoid becoming Peter II, was imprisoned and died here in 984.

Following Otto's death, the Crescentii clan ruled Rome. They now intervened again and had another 'John' installed. This John, i.e., XV (#138), was a son of a priest and a published scholar. He had been the cardinal priest at Rome's San Vitale. On January 31, 993, he became the first pope to officially canonize a Saint – viz. Ulrich, Bishop of Augsburg [Germany]. Three years earlier, he had curried favor with the Imperial family by acknowledging the legitimacy of Otto III's sovereignty as the King of Germany. Otto III was but three years old when he had been crowned as such just a few weeks after the sudden death of his father, Otto II [see above].

John XV liked to dabble in secular politics, both domestic and foreign, exploiting the then very fluid demarcation between state and Church. In the process, he gained a reputation that his motives in such dealings were mainly to increase his and his family's wealth and influence. Ten years into his papacy, he had become so isolated and held in such contempt by the local clergy that he had no option but to flee Rome. He sought refuge in Sutri [50 miles NW of

Rome] and pleaded with Otto III, now all of fifteen years of age, for help. Otto, with teenage aplomb, acquiesced, and set out for Rome in February of 966. To avoid the King's ire, the Romans persuaded the pope to return to the Lateran Palace. John was, however, to die from a nasty fever, in March, before Otto could get to Rome.

Gregory V (#139) : Otto III was in Northern Italy, on his way to Rome, responding to the beleaguered John XV's plea for aid, when he was informed that the pope had died. A delegation from Rome asked him to nominate the next pope – in part to show their contrition for their harsh treatment of John XV during the latter stages of his papacy.

Otto designated his personal chaplain, the 24 year old Bruno of Carinthia (the son of the Duke of Carinthia), who also happened to be his cousin. Bruno, accompanied by two German bishops, proceeded to Rome, where he was formally elected pope in early May 996. He was to be the first German-born pope, though not the first of Germanic origin. That distinction is believed to be held by Boniface II (#55), an Ostrogoth [an East Germanic tribe], born in Rome.

Bruno, who was well-educated, chose to be known as Gregory V, citing his admiration for the scholarly Gregory the Great (#64). It is believed that he changed his name to win favor with the Romans by not drawing attention to his German origins. This is the first instance where nationality was likely to have been the motive for a name change.

Figure 9: The enthronement of Otto III as the Holy Roman Emperor (996-1002) from the lavishly illuminated 'Gospels of Otto III' (based on the Vulgate) produced by the Reichenau Abbey [Germany] towards the end of the 10th century. Though not attributed, the 'bishop' shown on the Emperor's right may be Gregory V (#139) made to look older than the 24 years he was at that time.

Figure 10: Hadrian VI (#219), a carpenter's son from Utrecht [the Netherlands but then part of the Holy Roman Empire], who, as a noted scholar, went on to become the tutor of the future Holy Roman Emperor Charles V (1519-1556). Elected *in absentia* while acting as Charles' 'regent' in Spain, he opted to retain his birth name. He is portrayed here, during his papacy, by his compatriot Jan van Scorel – his appointee as an official Vatican painter.

Eighteen days after becoming pope, on Ascension Day, 21 May 996, he formally crowned his cousin Otto III as the Holy Roman Emperor at the Vatican. A month later, Otto, disliking Rome's summer heat, left Rome and headed back to Germany. Four months later, in October, Gregory was forced out of Rome at the instigation of the Crescentii family.

- *Name change became the norm following Gregory V.*

- The next 77 popes (counting Benedict IX but once, despite his three separate terms), over a 523 year period, each assumed a new name when elected.

- Hadrian VI (#219): Giovanni di Lorenzo de' Medici, the son of the Florentine Lorenzo "The Magnificent," was 37 years old when he became Leo X (#218). Though he is reputed to have claimed *"God has given us the papacy. Now let us enjoy it."*, the poise of his papacy was majorly buffeted by the rise of Martin Luther's Reformation. He was to die suddenly, of malaria, close to his 46th birthday in December 1521.

The conclave to select Leo's successor proved to be highly contentious. It was deadlocked 12 days after its start. Giulio di Giuliano de' Medici, Leo's cousin, conceded that neither he nor his friend Cardinal Alessandro Farnese had the requisite backing to be elected. He also pointed out that all of their opponents were unacceptable. He thus suggested that they seek a candidate who was not at the conclave – the Dutch, 63 year old, pro-Imperial Cardinal Adrian Florensz Dedal, who happened to be in Spain as the Holy Roman Emperor's 'regent.'

[Giulio Medici would succeed Hadrian as Clement VII (#220) while Cardinal Farnese would in turn succeed him as Paul III (#221).]

A delegation of three cardinals was sent to inform Cardinal Dedal of his election. He elected to retain his birth name and be known as Hadrian VI. The Romans were uneasy about his close association with the German Imperial court. Given that he originated from the North, they took to referring to him as a 'barbarian.' He is the only pope from the Netherlands and was the last non-Italian pope for 455 years until the election of John Paul II (#265).

ଔ Marcellus II (#223): Marcello Cervini degli Spannochi's father, a regional papal official, was also a chronologist who studied the stars. He believed that the stars foretold a promising career for his son within the Church. He thus encouraged Marcello to join the clergy at a young age. Well educated and erudite, Marcello became Paul III's (#221) papal secretary at the age of 33 and a cardinal at 38.

He was a co-president of the 1545 'session' of the influential 'Council of Trent' (1545-1563 in Northern Italy) that set out to rebut Protestantism. However, his tireless pursuit of Paul III's interests at this council displeased the Holy Roman Emperor Charles V. He was thus not in contention as a successor to Paul, given that his name was included in Charles' list of unacceptable candidates. Julius III (#222) thus succeeded Paul III.

The hurried conclave, convened eleven days after Julius' death, was only attended by 37 (~65%) of the eligible cardinals – 30 of those attending being Italian. Marcello was not explicitly excluded by Charles this time around. Consequently, he was 'unanimously' elected on the fourth day, via a written ballot, with Marcello supposedly initiating the tradition whereby the presumptive winner casts his vote for the Dean of the College of Cardinals rather than for himself. Marcello decided to retain his birth name.

Noted for his integrity and zeal, there were high hopes that this pope would enact much needed positive reforms. He started well by having a modest coronation (apropos given that it was during Lent) and taking steps to reduce the size of his court. But the celebrations related to Easter proved too much for the new pope, who was supposedly somewhat frail, though relatively young at 54 years of age. He died 22 days after his election, and is now best known as the last pope to have retained his birth name.

A MORE CRITICAL HISTORY OF PAPAL NAME CHANGE

The problem with the conventional history of papal name change, as outlined above, is its lack of precision, which compromises the veracity of some of its claims. Many of the oversights appear to be due to inadequate attention being paid to the exact meaning of Italian birth names. Thus, 'Giuliano' being but an Italian variant of 'Julius' is overlooked as is the correlation between 'Giovanni' and 'John.' Consequently, the emphasis given to Hadrian VI (#219) as the pope who ended the longest run of continuous papal name changes is misplaced – for a start.

Shortening the longest run of name changes at both ends

Julius II (#217), one pope ahead of Hadrian, also retained his birth name – viz. 'Giuliano.' But this gets overlooked, since the names look different at first glance. Ironically, there is also a corresponding problem at the start of this long run. Papal name change was not to be the norm following Gregory V (#139). The pope who followed Gregory did indeed change his name from Gerbert to Silvester II (#140). But the next two popes both retained their birth names, viz. 'John!'

Figure 11: Julius II (#217), who by retaining his birth name 'Giuliano,' ended the longest run of successive papal name changes – 19 years prior to Hadrian VI (#219) retaining his birth name. He is depicted here by Raphael, whom he had commissioned to decorate his new papal apartments while Michelangelo was being coerced to beautify the Sistine Chapel ceiling.

The ever ambitious Crescentii family had been instrumental in deposing John XIV (#137), installing John XV (#138) and temporarily expelling Gregory V (#139) from Rome. With Otto III's unexpected death in 1002, most likely from malaria, they again wrested control of Rome. Thus, when Silvester II died in May 1003, John II Crescentius, the new head of the family, determined who would be the next pope. He put forward a Roman named John Sicco, whose father was also a John.

20 years, 6 popes, 4 named 'John'

The Crescentiis do appear to have been partial to the name 'John.' Whether through coincidence or otherwise, three of the four popes selected by the Crescentiis bore the name 'John' -- the one exception being Sergius IV (#143).

[John XIII (#134), contrary to widespread claims, is unlikely to have been a Crescenti. Particularly so given his close ties to the Holy Roman Emperor – the nemesis of the Crescentiis.]

JOHNS: 965 TO 1009

#134	John XIII	965-972
#137	John XIV 'Pietro'	983-984
UNDOCUMENTED JOHN [p. 84]		
#138	John XV	985-996
ANTIPOPE JOHN (XVI)		997-998
#141	John XVII 'Sicco'	1003-1003
#142	John XVIII (XIX) 'Fasanus'	1003-1009

Little is reliably known about John Sicco, who became John XVII (#141). It is said that he was a priest who had been previously married and had fathered three sons. His was to be a brief papacy just short of six months.

In reality he should have been John XVI rather than XVII.

In February 997 John Philagathos, at the instigation of the Crescentiis, had himself elected as John XVI. Gregory V (#139), however, was still pope – albeit in exile in Northern Italy. A year later, Philagathos was deemed an antipope (and brutally mutilated) when Otto III accompanied his cousin Gregory back to Rome. Five years later, when Sicco was being installed, there should not have been any question that Philagathos had been an antipope. Sicco, as the next legitimate 'John,' should have repossessed the XVI. But this did not happen, thereby irrevocably disrupting the numbering sequence for the subsequent 'Johns.'

At Sicco's death, John II Crescentius next turned to Giovani (John) Fasanus, then the cardinal priest of St. Peter's, who may have been a relative. He became John XVIII – though in time some chroniclers started to refer to him as John XIX or John XVIII (XIX).

This bump up in sequence numbers was prompted by the belief that there was a phantom pope in between John XIV's (#137) eviction in April 984 and the installation of John XV (#138) a year later. Amazingly, this undocumented pope was also thought to have been a 'John,' which would have been the only instance of three consecutive popes with the same name. This enigma is cleared up on page 84.

Antipope Boniface who displaced the first 'John' was, however, acting as pope in Rome during most of this time. Given the anarchic turbulence pervading Rome at that time, it was indeed plausible to believe that some Roman faction did legitimately elect another 'pope' to counter Boniface. But this all proved to be a misunderstanding. The anomalies in the numberings of the 'Johns' following XV are dealt with in chapter IV.

During his five-and-a-half year pontificate, John XVIII forcefully dealt with diocesan normalization matters in Germany and French bishops who were coveting local abbeys. He also tried to improve relations with the new Holy Roman Emperor, Henry II (1014-1024) and with Constantinople; the Crescentiis discouraged the former but aided in the latter. He is known to have died in mid-1009.

A sarcophagus at Rome's St. Paul's Outside the Walls (San Paolo fuori le Mura) bears his papal name. But his name also appears, at the very top of column 3, on the marble tablet in St. Peter's listing the popes buried there. Many respected sources, though, believe that he spent his last days at St. Paul's. If so, he was most likely forced out of the Vatican.

The Crescentiis next turned to Pietro 'Bucca Porci,' the Bishop of Albano [Italy]. He was the second 'Pietro' to be *elected* pope (obviously excluding St. Peter whose status was never contingent on election). He chose to be known as Sergius IV (#143) to avoid being 'Peter.' He may have chosen 'Sergius' to denote his firm allegiance to the Crescentiis given that St. Sergius I (#84) was noted for having defied Imperial interference.

The long run of successive papal name changes that was ended by Julius II (#217) thus started with Sergius IV. The next 71 (as opposed to 77) popes changed their names over a 494 year (rather than a 523 year) period.

'Anacletus' may have been the first name change

Anacletus (#3), denoting blameless, and Sixtus I (#7), for 6th after St. Peter, were, as earlier discussed, inordinately auspicious names for two early popes. It is also, however, significant that there were transformations, 'Cletus' and 'Xystus' respectively, associated with both these two names. The transformations, luckily, shed some light onto the possible provenance of these two names.

The current belief is that 'Cletus' is just a shortened form of 'Anacletus.' If so, it does appear somewhat incongruous that such a contraction, in essence a nickname, would be used in something as revered as the list of martyrs celebrated at Mass. Particularly so, given the relevance and gravitas of the original name.

One could conjecture that 'Cletus' may have been a ruse to avoid drawing attention to the 'blameless' or 'former slave' connotations of 'Anacletus.' But that does seem kind of farfetched especially for that era. Being an ex-slave was not a major stigma and there is at least one well documented instance of an ex-slave who became a pope – viz. St. Callistus I (#16).

At a time with no mass media and limited access to bibles, it is unlikely that there would have been much skepticism about an early bishop whose name happened to echo St. Paul's stated criteria for that office. In addition, it is known that there was confusion that there had in fact been two separate popes, one of Greek origin named 'Anacletus' and another a Roman named 'Cletus.' So any possible attempts to disguise 'Anacletus' obviously had not succeeded.

Given these disconnects, it is valid and equally plausible to contend that maybe 'Cletus' was the birth name, and either the pope or church historians expanded it to be 'Anacletus' to portray the pope as blameless. It may even have happened during his papacy (rather than at the start) or even after his death (but before c. 175 given that Irenaeus refers of him as 'Anacletus'). By today's standards, at least this reversed hypothesis would better explain why he is referred to in the Mass as 'Cletus,' and the confusion as to the existence of two different popes.

The bottom line here is that there is definitely some basis to suppose that the name by which the fourth Bishop of Rome is known by may not have been his real birth (or priestly) name.

'Xystus' was probably assumed; 'Sixtus' was spin-doctoring?

In the case of Sixtus I (#7), it would definitely appear that his original name was 'Xystus' per well regarded sources such as the 1917 *'Catholic Encyclopedia,'* *'Oxford Dictionary of Popes'* and *Liber Pontificalis* (Book of the Popes). Some now claim that 'Xystus' is but a variant of 'Sixtus.' But this appears to be a *post factum* accommodation prompted by the papal name transpositions.

'Xystus' is Greek. 'Sixtus' is Latin – though the regnal name in this case is the Greek 'Xystus.' Most of the 1st and 2nd century popes, 11 out of 14 to be precise, had Greek names – Clement, Pius and Victor being the exceptions. But only five of the 11 with Greek names are believed to be of Greek origin – and with at least two of these the supposition of their 'Greekness' is based on their Greek names!

P.G. Maxwell-Stuart in *'Chronicle of the Popes,'* suggests that the Latin name 'Sixtus' thus bucks the prevailing trend. Maxwell-Stuart is also one of the few to openly question whether the early popes assumed Greek names to emulate St. Peter's name change – 'Petrus' being the Greek rendering of the Aramaic word for 'rock.'

'Xystus' is derived from, or a corrupted version of, the Greek 'xustos' that means 'smooth' or 'polished.' As such, it is also said to connote 'shaved.' It is used, in addition, in the context of Greek architecture to refer to a covered porch that permits *al fresco* exercise during inclement weather. The Romans appear to have extrapolated this usage to include garden walkways installed in front of a porch. In both these instances, the term may still hark back to its original sense in describing a 'smooth' (or polished) surface.

It is noteworthy that *Liber Pontificalis,* which started as a compilation of papal names in the 3rd century, lists the 6th pope after St. Peter as Xystus I. However, Irenaeus, when writing *Adversus Haereses* just 50-60 years after this papacy glibly refers to Sixtus, the sixth from the apostles, with no caveats or mention of Xystus. Consequently, one has no choice but to assume that 'Sixtus' was the result of 'spin doctoring' by early church

Figure 12: A Roman 'crown' tonsure of the type thought to have been popularized by St. Peter. 'Xystus' may have been a reference to such tonsures and thereby a name denoting priesthood. The figure depicted here is from Fra Angelico's monastery of San Marco fresco *'Mocking of Christ.'*

historians who wanted to imbue an element of Providence to papal succession – via what was essentially a *pun*.

'Xystus,' with its allusion to 'shaved' and thus 'tonsured,' however, may itself have been an assumed name! St. Peter is believed to have popularized the Roman 'crown' tonsure where the top of the head was shaved and the remaining hair shaped to look like laurel wreath. Thus a tonsure was probably a mark of distinction in the early Roman church.

Some priests, on ordination, once tonsured may have assumed the name 'Xystus' to emphasize their new role in life. This would be consistent with the biblical tradition of name change following a marked change in spiritual status – as with papal name change. That would certainly explain why 'Xystus/Sixtus' was the most prevalent of the papal names during the first 500 years of papal history.

There were to be three popes named 'Xystus/Sixtus,' i.e., #7, #24 and #44, before any other name was to be repeated. Felix II, who at one point was told to be 'co-pope,' is deemed an antipope as discussed in the side bar on page 46.

It is conceivable that devout parents who wanted their newborn son to become a priest preordained it by naming him 'Xystus' – envisioning the day when he would be tonsured. It is also possible, though considerably less likely, that some whimsical parents amused by the birth of a particularly hairless boy would name him 'Xystus.' Likewise, one cannot ignore the likelihood that 'Xystus,' rather than being either an assumed or a birth name, was instead a tenacious nickname earned by 'follically challenged' adult males or those that defied prevailing social customs by not growing a beard. To this end, Maxwell-Stuart in *'Chronicle of the Popes'* points out that the Roman Emperor during Xystus I's time, Hadrian (117-138), had reversed a long standing trend by popularizing beards. Hadrian, however, came to power around the time Xystus I was elected. Thus, Hadrian, *per se*, might not have been a factor here.

The bottom line here is that Sixtus I appears to have been a name concocted by early church propagandists to stress the role of Providence in papal succession. 'Xystus' may also not have been his birth name. Instead, it was probably his clerical name. That his feast day is April 6 emphasizes this 6th related theme.

The 1917 *'Catholic Encyclopedia'* explicitly states that 'Xystus' was the original 'spelling' used to denote the first three popes now known as 'Sixtus.' One has to thus assume that, at a minimum, the names of Xystus II and III were altered, at a later date, for consistency with Sixtus I. Sixtus IV and V, however, assumed that name. IV because the conclave that elected him convened on the feast day of Sixtus II while V did so because IV had been a fellow Franciscan [p. 89-90].

Though not as marked, St. Evaristus (#5), too, may have been the beneficiary of some inspired name embellishment. As with 'Anacletus,' (a.k.a. 'Cletus') many sources, even today, list 'Aristus' as another name by which 'Evaristus' was known by. The 1917 *'Catholic Encyclopedia'* states that he is known as 'Aristus' in the *'Liberian Catalogue.'* This is a listing of the popes, believed to have been complied in the 4th century, that culminates with Pope Liberius (#36) – hence its name.

Given the above postulations on Anacletus and Sixtus I, it is no longer possible to just dismiss 'Aristus' as being but an insignificant contraction. Instead, it would appear to be another intentional Latin to Greek transposition. 'Aristus' in Latin describes the appearance of grain. It connotes harvesting. Thus, it was an appropriate name for somebody born during the harvest. It is also believed to be an Italian variant of 'Aristotle,' the Romans being rather familiar with the c. 350 BC Greek philosopher. So, as with Sixtus I, there could have been a slight change to the original Latin name to make it into an engaging Greek name befitting a pope.

Italian popes with Greek names – one even allegorical?

During the first century, Latin and Greek demarcated the farflung Roman Empire. In the Eastern half Greek was used, by and large, for trade, civic governance, formal correspondence and cultural exposition. Latin ruled the West. Hebrew, the formal language of the Old Testament, was the means for Jewish religious rituals and learning. Aramaic was the vernacular of Jesus and his Holy Land contemporaries, with Greek the *lingua franca* for cross-regional interactions. Consequently, Jews moving from Palestine to other regions, such as Rome, resorted to Greek to communicate with their new neighbors.

Greek was the mother-tongue of St. Paul, who is said to have been born in Tarsus [in today's Turkey]. St. Paul's letters, all written in Greek (many by scribes), were some of the earliest of Christian writings. They were to become the earliest books of the New Testament. The Gospel of Mark, thought to have been completed around 70 AD, was originally written in Greek.

Greek, therefore, was the religious language of the early Church – even in Rome. Consequently, it is to be expected that assumed Greek names, such as 'Xystus' and 'Soter' (savior), may have been favored by priests joining the new Church, even if they were native Italians – particularly since 'Petrus' was also Greek.

All twelve of the popes that succeeded St. Linus (#2), spanning the 1st and the entire 2nd century, had illustrious names – nine of them Greek. If 'Linus,' which is also Greek, is interpreted as 'golden' as opposed to the more mundane 'flaxen haired,' one could claim that all 1st and 2nd century popes had distinguished names and that eleven of these were Greek – including St. Petrus. Refer to Appendices A and B.

The name of the first 3rd century pope, St. Zephyrinus (#15), rather than being distinguished *per se* could have been allegorical. 'Zephyr' refers to the west wind. By the middle of the 1st century, the churches in the East and West were beginning to have divergent convictions. As to when Easter should be celebrated was the initial bone of contention. To begin with, under St. Anicetus (#11), negotiations about adopting standard practices were cordial and conciliatory.

But after 30 years of vacillation, St. Victor I (#14) set out to impose Rome's will on the Eastern churches. He insisted that they too, like the

Figure 13: 'Zephyr,' the Greek god of the west wind, shown here in Sandro Botticelli's timeless *La Primavera* (as the one reaching down). Did the 15th pope, believed to be a Roman, assume the Greek name 'Zephyrinus' as an allegorical reference to the West's hoped for ascendancy over the Eastern church? Rome, on the matter of when Easter should be celebrated, was trying to get the Eastern bishops to follow pope's lead.

West, celebrate Easter on the Sunday after the Jewish Passover – rather than on the eve of the Passover. Bishops in the East, such as Polycrates the Bishop of Ephesus [Turkey], demurred in agreeing to the pope's request. St. Victor excommunicated them. Though it did not result in a schism, probably because Western bishops urged Victor to relent, relations between the East and West were sullied and strained.

This contretemps over Easter was the first instance of a pope trying to exert his powers far beyond the see of Rome. It was the initial seed sown towards the assertion of papal primacy. Victor was pope for around 10 years. Prior to being elected pope, Zephyrinus is believed to have been a senior Roman presbyter or possibly even a bishop of a Roman suburb for over 20 years. Thus, he would have to have been an associate of Victor's, *au fait* with his thinking; he was possibly even a confidant.

The crux of Victor's papacy was the West's desire to bring about change in the East. The new pope elected just happens to allude to a propagation of this theme by having a name that conveys winds (of change) from the West. As with Sixtus I, one could say that this too was but providential. But it could equally have been a judiciously selected assumed name.

St. Fabian (#20) is the first pope to have a rather pedestrian name – Latin at that. Eusebius of Caesarea, sometimes credited as being the father of Church history, wrote about Fabian's election. He claims that

Figure 14: St. Fabian (#20), on left, with St. Sebastian in a painting by 15th century Sienese painter Giovanni di Paolo (now at the National Gallery, London). Fabian, probably the first layman to be elected pope, just also happens to be the first with a non-distinguished name. Does this suggest that Roman clergy regularly assumed new priestly names upon ordination?

when Roman clergy and some laity convened to elect Anterus' (#19) successor, a dove, signifying the Holy Spirit, alighted on Fabian's head. Fabian, who had not been a contender, and might even have been a bean farmer per his name, was then immediately elected by acclamation. He could thus have been the first layman to be elected pope.

Subsequently, the first non-distinguished papal name occurs with the first possible election of a layman. As with Sixtus I and Zephyrinus, to dismiss this as being nothing more than a coincidence would be injudicious. Though obviously not conclusive, it, however, lends some credence to the hypothesis that early Roman priests, if not the early popes, assumed new names when their station in life changed.

The two popes that succeeded Fabian also had Latin names -- one distinguished the other nondescript. Prior to this, there had been no instance of successive popes having Latin names. But with Fabian, St. Cornelius (#21) and Lucius (#22), there were suddenly three popes in a row with Latin names. In essence, two hundred years after St. Peter, the popularity of Greek names start to wane.

The 5th century is dominated by popes with Latin names – with St. Anastasius I and II (#39 & #50) being the notable exceptions; 'Anastasius' being Greek for resurrected. Hebrew names, viz. John and Symmachus, came to be in the 6th century, which also saw the first two documented names changes: i.e., Mercurius and Catelinus. By now, names such as Mark, John, Felix and Boniface were beginning to get reused.

In the 7th century, most of the names were Latin or ones that were being reused with just a smattering with Greek origins – most notably 'Theodore' (God's gift) and 'Agatho' (good). There were no new Greek names used in the 8th century. 'Nicholas,' in 858, was to be the last new Greek name. Appropriately, it belonged to St. Nicholas I the Great (#106), the third and last of the three popes to be known as Great.

Distinguished names and those that recur

Nearly half of the 81 elemental papal names have illustrious meanings – whether their origins are Greek, Latin or Hebrew. The most noteworthy of these, divided by language, being:

GREEK

▶ Blameless (Anacletus)

▶ Savior (Soter)

▶ Devout (Eusebius)

▶ Beloved (Agapetus)

▶ Resurrection (Anastasius)

▶ Fortunate (Eutychian)

▶ Accomplished (Telesphorus)

▶ Pleasing (Evaristus)

▶ Unconquered (Anicetus)

▶ Tonsured → priest (Xystus)

▶ Defender of men (Alexander)

▶ Watchful (vigilant) (Gregory)

▶ Victory of the people (Nicholas)

LATIN

▶ Guiltless (Pure) (Innocent)

▶ Bringer of light (Lucius)

▶ Dutiful (Pius)

▶ Rejoice (Caius)

▶ Blessed (Benedict)

▶ Fortunate (Boniface)

▶ Honorable (Honorius)

▶ Heavenly (Celestine)

▶ Champion (Victor)

▶ Steadfast (Constantine)

▶ Strong & vigorous (Valentine)

▶ Vigilant (Vigilius)

▶ Firm or stern (Severinus)

LATIN (CONTINUED)

▶ Servant of Christ (Sergius)

▶ Humble (Paul)

▶ He who is good (Simplicius)

▶ Joyful (Hilarius)

▶ Bright (Gelasius)

▶ Free (Liberius)

HEBREW

▶ God is gracious (John)

▶ God has remembered (Zacharius)

▶ Joy (Symmachus)

All of the 30 assumed papal names, with the singular exception of 'John Paul,' are considered to have first entered the papal rolls as supposed birth (or prior) names. Consequently, per conventional papal history, none of the illustrious names can be rationalized as being auspicious names chosen by a pope elect. Quite a few of these illustrious names also recurred as birth (prior) names before assumed names became the trend. There were even instances of successive popes with the same illustrious birth name: e.g., John VI & VII (#85 & #86), Gregory II & III (#89 & #90) and Benedict VI & VII (#134 & #135).

'Stephen,' Greek for 'crown' and thus denoting 'kingship,' is another name that can be classed as being distinguished – though it is also revered as that of the *Protomartyr* (first martyr) of Christianity. It is considered to be the birth name of nine first millennium popes – four within a span of 65 years and eight within 188 years. Since then, there has only been one other pope with that birth name; viz. Étienne Aubert, the French variant of the name, who became Innocent VI (#200).

The clustered occurrences of 'Stephen' could be coincidental. It could have been a popular birth name during that era. But this clustering, however, also bears a marked resemblance to how assumed names such as Pius, Clement and Benedict were reused during the latter half of the second millennium.

The bottom line here is that there are, in essence, three explanations for the high number of illustrious names among the first 140 popes. These being:

1. All these popes had refined, discerning and devout parents that gave them lofty, sometimes even prescient, names – possibly even naming some in honor of a pope.

2. Some priests, emulating at a minimum St. Paul, assumed new priestly names on being ordained – particularly so if their birth names lacked sufficient gravitas.

3. Many more popes than previously thought assumed new names upon being elected to either emulate Saints Peter and Paul, to get rid of an incongruous birth name or signify allegiance with the piety or politics of a prior pope.

The devout parent explanation, indubitably, accounts for some of the illustrious names. The presence of some beholden names such as Theodore, Donus and Deusdedit (all alluding to God's benevolence), Formosus (beautiful), Vitalian (full of life), Hyginus (healthy) and Eugene (well born), add weight to this supposition. But names like Sergius (servant of Christ), Xystus (shaved/tonsured) and Eusebius (devout), tend to suggest that at least some of the illustrious papal names may have been assumed. If some priests and popes did assume new names, that would also explain the multiple recurrences of some of the illustrious names.

'Catelinus,' who became John III (#61), is regarded as only the second pope to have assumed a new name. But he may have already been 'John' when he was elected pope – having assumed that name when he became a subdeacon. This may be the final clue as to the possibility of 'priestly' names. Pelagius I (#60), John's predecessor, started translating the 5th century *'Saying of the Elders'* from Greek to Latin while he was still a deacon.

The *'Oxford Dictionary of Popes'* and a few Web sites (e.g., holytrinitymission.org) mention that a subdeacon named 'John' assisted Pelagius. The *'Oxford Dictionary of Popes'* asserts that John III probably was that subdeacon. Tellingly, it also does not mention a papal name change. Instead, it just says that 'Catelinus' was his original name. Could this mean that 'Catelinus' became John not when he became pope but when he joined the clergy?

The critical history of papal name change vis-à-vis the conventional

CRITICAL HISTORY	CONVENTIONAL HISTORY
▶ Cletus ('summoned') becomes the 'blameless' Anacletus (#3)?	
▶ Aristus (to do with grain) gets changed to Evaristus (#5) – Greek for 'pleasing'?	
▶ Xystus ('tonsured'), the sixth in-line after St. Peter, is portrayed as Sixtus I (#7) – indicating the 6th?	

/continued

<table>
<tr><td>

CRITICAL HISTORY
(CONTINUED I)

</td><td>

CONVENTIONAL HISTORY
(CONTINUED I)

</td></tr>
</table>

CRITICAL HISTORY (CONTINUED I) — CONVENTIONAL HISTORY (CONTINUED I)

▶ Of the next 7 popes, 6 had illustrious names suggesting the possibility of some assumed names.

▶ Was Zephyrinus (#15), denoting the west wind, an assumed allegorical name to indicate Rome's wish to bring about change in the East?

▶ Fabian (#20), thought to be the first layman to be elected pope, also happens to have the first non-distinguished name – suggesting a correlation between priests and distinguished names.

▶ Continued occurrence of illustrious names suggests the possibility of some assumed names.

▶ Mercurius, deciding to be known as John II (#53), is probably just the first documented instance of a papal name change.

▶ John II (#53) is the first pope to change his name.

▶ Catelinus might have assumed the name 'John' when he was made a subdeacon – as opposed to when he was elected pope.

▶ John III (#61) is the second pope to change his name.

▶ Some of the illustrious names begin to recur, regularly, suggesting some assumed names – with some new popes signaling their affinity with prior popes.

/continued

CRITICAL HISTORY	CONVENTIONAL HISTORY
(CONTINUED II)	(CONTINUED II)

▶ Octavian changes his name to become John XIII (#131).

▶ John III (#131) is the third pope to change his name.

▶ Pietro Canepanova changes his name to John XIV (#137) to avoid becoming Peter II.

▶ Pietro Canepanova changes his name to John XIV (#137) to avoid becoming Peter II.

▶ Bruno of Carinthia, the first German *born* pope, becomes Gregory V (#139) to avoid drawing attention to his nationality.

▶ Bruno of Carinthia, the first German pope, becomes Gregory V (#139) to avoid drawing attention to his nationality.

▶ Popes #141 and #142 retain their birth name, viz. 'John.'

▶ *Name changes becomes the norm after Gregory V (#139).*

▶ The next 72 popes, over a 494 year period, changed their names.

▶ *The next 77 popes, over a 523 year period, changed their names.*

▶ Giuliano della Rovere retains his birth name to become Julius II (#217).

▶ Adrian Florensz retains his birth name to become Hadrian VI (#219).

▶ Adrian Florensz retains his birth name to become Hadrian VI (#219).

▶ Marcello Spannochi retains his birth name to become Marcellus II (#223) – the last pope, to-date, to have retained his birth name.

▶ Marcello Spannochi retains his birth name to become Marcellus II (#223) – the last pope, to-date, to have retained his birth name.

FELIX II – THE 3ᴿᴰ ANTIPOPE

If Felix II had been a legitimate pope, 'Xystus/Sixtus' would not have occurred three times before any other papal name was repeated. Instead, Felix II would have preceded Xystus/Sixtus III (#44). 'Felix,' nonetheless, would still be the next name after that of 'Xystus/Sixtus' to be repeated, but that was with Felix III (#48) 51 years after Xystus/Sixtus III.

Felix II was yet another unintended casualty of the Arian controversy that so disrupted Christiandom during the 4th century. It was initiated by Arius, an influential priest from Alexandria [Egypt], who, in essence, questioned the divinity of Christ. This proved to be extremely divisive. So much so that Constantine, the Emperor who in 313 legalized Christianity, felt obliged to intervene. He, in 325, convened the Council of Nicaea [Turkey], with the primary goal of resolving this roiling controversy.

This council, attended by upwards of 300 bishops, resoundingly condemned the views of Arius [i.e., Arianism]. It was agreed that 'of one being' was the relationship between the Father and the Son. One of the leaders of the anti-Arius faction at Nicaea was Athanasius, the bishop of Alexandria.

Constantine died in 337. Constantius II, his second son, rose to power. He was an ardent pro-Arian. So much so, that he wanted Liberius (#36), who had been elected in 352, to condemn and exile Athanasius. Liberius demurred. For this defiance, he was deposed and exiled by the Emperor in 355. The Emperor appointed Felix, a Roman archdeacon, as the new bishop. He became Felix II.

The appointment of Felix II was controversial. It contravened an oath taken by all the Roman clergy not to accept an alternate to Liberius while he was still alive. Ironically, it appears that this oath was Felix's idea in the first place!

Liberius was in exile for more than two years. During that time, he agreed, under duress, to compromise on his stance on Arianism. There was also a clamor by the Romans for his return. Constantius agreed to this on the proviso that he would rule jointly with Felix II. This was not to be. Felix saw the warm welcome afforded to Liberius by the Romans on his return. Rather than compete with Liberius, he left Rome, despite claiming, till his death in November 365, his right to that bishopric.

III:
TRENDS IN
PAPAL NAMES

hen it comes to papal name trends one of the most striking is the compactness, constancy and constrictiveness of the pool of names. It is also very much a tale of two millenniums – evenly divided. Only one new name was added to the papal name pool during the entirety of the 2nd millennium. That being 'John Paul' (#264) in 1978. Hence, 80 of the 81 papal names were initially used during the 1st millennium. Only 31 elemental names in total were used during the 2nd millennium – all but 'John Paul' from the prior millennium.

There were only five *documented* name changes in the 1st millennium. There were 119 in the 2nd. Only 4% of popes were *known* to change their name during the 1st millennium. 94% did so in the 2nd.

'Stephen,' occurring nine times, was the second most prevalent name in the first millennium. It only occurred once in the 2nd! 'Clement,' with thirteen occurrences, was the most prevalent 2nd millennium name. It only occurred once in the 1st millennium – it having been the name of the fourth pope, c.90. It is, by a thin whisker, the most popular assumed name – both absolutely as well as relatively. It was assumed a total of thirteen times – the most for any name. But since there have only been fourteen popes named 'Clement,' its popularity [or relativity] 'quotient' [i.e., assumed/total] is 92.9%. Per this metric 'John Paul,' the only name that was never a birth name, gets a 100% popularity 'quotient' [p. 70-72].

'Gregory' and 'Innocent' were each assumed twelve times. But there were sixteen 'Gregorys' and thirteen 'Innocents.' Thus, the popularity 'quotient' for 'Innocent' comes in at 92.3%, while that for 'Gregory' is 75%. Eleven of the twelve popes named 'Pius' assumed that name. Therefore, 'Pius' has the third highest popularity 'quotient' at 91.7% .

'Innocent,' 'Pius' and 'Clement' were three of the four most widely used papal names during the 2nd millennium. Each, however, only occurred once as a birth (or possibly priestly) name – all in the 1st millennium. Hence, every occurrence of these names in the 2nd millennium was due to a name change. 'Gregory,' the 3rd most popular name during the 2nd millennium, did occur four times as a birth (or priestly) name– but again all of these four instances being in the 1st millennium.

'John,' the most prevalent of the names, occurred fifteen times between 523 and 996, but only six times after that. There were seven popes named 'John' in a 182 year period between 523 and 705. But 624 years and 64 popes separated the last two popes to use that name, viz. John XXII (#197) and Blessed John XXIII (#262), albeit with an early 15th century antipope John (XXIII) in between.

During the 1st millennium, there were eleven pope-elects whose names were 'John' – be it as a birth name or possibly an assumed priestly name. During the 2nd millennium, there were to be nineteen popes whose birth names were known to be 'John' (or the Italian 'Giovanni'). But here is the twist. All eleven of the 1st millennium 'Johns' had retained their prior name. But only two of the nineteen did so during the 2nd millennium and both of those in the very early days of the 11th century.

The longest run of uninterrupted papal name changes started after those two 11th century 'Johns,' viz. John (Sicco) XVII (#141) and John (Fasanus) XVIII (XIX) (#142). Subsequent to Givoanni Fasanus, all seventeen other

Figure 15: Blessed John XXIII (#262), beloved, influential and warmhearted, the last pope to-date to be 'John.' The name had not been used for 624 years. 'John Paul' pays homage to him. As the pope who convened the Vatican II council, he is considered to have been progressive by some conservatives. But his popularity ensures that a future John XXIV is a distinct possibility.

pope-elects with the birth name 'John' opted to assume names such as Pius (x3), Innocent (x2), Clement (x2) and Paul (x2). But four popes, with birth names 'Romanus,' 'Pedro,' 'Jacques' and 'Angelo,' assumed the name John. The ebb and flow in the popularity of the name 'John' is further discussed later in this chapter.

The clustered popularity of 'Pius'

Seven of the last sixteen popes [i.e., from #251 to Benedict XVI at #266] assumed the name 'Pius.' That means that 44% of the popes elected during the last 233 years wished to be known as 'Pius.' During this period, there were two instances of successive popes bearing that name [i.e., #251 & 252 and #260 & 261]. There was also never more than one intervening pope in between the succession of those called 'Pius.' It was quite a trend, though now severed by a quintet of popes who preferred other names.

All but one of these seven popes named 'Pius' enjoyed papacies considerably longer than the average. The average for all 265 popes is a tad over seven years. Pius VIII (#254) reigned but one year and eight months. The next shortest reign for this select group is eleven years. That was that of St. Pius X (#258), the last pope to be canonized to date. He was the first to be so honored since St. Pius V (#226), who died in 1572.

Pius IX (#256), whose papacy lasted 31 years and 7 months, is the longest serving pope to date. Pius VI's (#251) reign was the 4th longest,

Figure 16: The coat of arms of Pope St. Pius X (#258) – the last pope to be canonized to date and the first pope to be canonized since the 16th century Pius V (#226). The lion of St. Mark at the top symbolizes his tenure as Patriarch of Venice from 1893 to when he was elected pope in 1903. The anchor at the bottom alludes to *"Which hope we have as an anchor of the soul ..."* from Hebrews 6:19. This was carried over from his coat of arms when he was Bishop of Mantua [Italy] from 1884 to 1893.

Figure 17: Pope St. Pius V (#226) devout and committed to church reform but considered harsh and too reliant on the Inquisition. Nonetheless, canonized 140 years after his death for his leadership. Shown here in a portrait attributed to the Cretan-born El Greco – best known for his work in Toledo, Spain. El Greco did meet Pius V in Rome c. 1570. He offered to obliterate Michelangelo's *Last Judgment* in the Sistine Chapel by painting over it given that the Pope and a few others were discomfited by the nude figures.

while that of Pius VII (#252) was the 6th longest. These seven popes, in total, thus held office for over 129 years (for an average of 18.4 years between them). Consequently, between 1775 and 2005, a pope named 'Pius' was at the Vatican for more than half of the time.

During this lengthy period of 'Pius' domination the only other name that occurred more than once was 'John Paul.' However, prior to gaining this popularity, 'Pius' had had a 203 year hiatus during which 24 popes opted for other names – Clement (x7), Innocent (x5) and Gregory (x3) being the favorites. This hiatus occurred immediately after the first successive use of 'Pius' [i.e., Pius IV (#225) & V (#226)]. It is possible that Pius V, a Dominican, though much admired for his piety and his zeal to reform the Church, was perceived as being intolerant and harsh – particularly so given his long-term association with and partiality to the Inquisition.

But Pius V was nonetheless beatified in 1672 and canonized 40 years later by Clement XI (#244). Pius VI (#251) assumed the name 63 years later to rekindle its popularity. Prior to Pius V, popes had favored red cassocks similar to those worn by cardinals. Pius, who had become a Dominican at the age of fourteen, preferred wearing the white cassock associated with that order. Popes that succeeded Pius V continued his tradition of wearing white cassocks – augmented, on occasion, with a red cape that evoked the old papal colors.

Popes that assumed the name 'Clement' dominated the 18th century. They made up four out of the total of eight popes [i.e., 50%] – with one instance of successive usage [i.e., Clement XIII (#249) & XIV (#250)]. With Clement XI's [#244] papacy lasting 20 years and 4 months, these four 'Clements' between them held office for 45.5 years during that century.

The occurrences of 'Innocent' and 'Gregory,' the second and joint-third of the most popular 2nd millennium names, were, in general, more spaced out than those of 'Pius' and 'Clement.' For a start, neither was *assumed* by successive popes. [The one instance of 'Gregory' occurring consecutively was in the 8th century, II [#89] and III [#90] – with birth names.] The only cluster being the three 'Innocents' between September 1676 and March 1724, viz. Innocent XI (#241), XII (#243) and XIII (#245).

Trying to dissect the trends

The sections *'Trends in papal names by 250 year blocks'* and *'Trends in papal names by century'* in this chapter provide a detailed and granular breakdown of name usage and name change patterns. These tables show, for a start, that there has yet to be a chronological half-millennium during which name change was 100%.

They also show how the popes over the centuries have converged on increasingly smaller subsets of names. Hence, the constrictiveness of the name pool. During the 18th and 19th centuries, the popes-to-names ratio was 2:1. During the 18th century, eight popes used four names, while in the 19th, six popes used three names. That is a far cry from, say, the 9th century when 21 popes used 16 names, i.e., 1.3:1 ratio.

This ratio was 1:1 during the first 250 years. The first name to be repeated, i.e., Xystus/Sixtus II (#24), occurred in August of 257. This ratio has since increased to the point that it was 4.06:1 for the 2nd millennium, i.e., the same name shared by four popes. Overall, for all 266 popes, the ratio is 3.27:1, i.e., 266 popes using 81 names between them.

There were also three other hard to ignore trends over the last half millennium:

1. Increasingly firmer commitment to upholding the tradition of name change to signify the marked new role in life embarked upon by a pope-elect. During the 16th century, three popes, in relatively quick succession, opted to retain their birth names. But since then, 48 other popes have solemnly adhered to the tradition. Among these were those with names such as 'Giovanni' ('John'), Alessandro ('Alexander'), Giulio ('Julius'), 'Felice' ('Felix'), 'Niccolò' (Nicholas), 'Fabio' ('Fabian') and 'Eugenio' ('Eugene'). Any of them, per 'Giovanni' (#142),

'Guiliano' (#217), 'Adrian' (#219) or 'Marcello' (#223), could have easily justified retaining their birth name. Instead, they all bowed to tradition.

2. Inclination of pope elects to assume a name from a small core group of venerated names, viz. Pius, Clement, Innocent, Gregory, Leo and Paul. Fifteen names were used by the 50 popes during 1503 to 2005 with these five names occurring a total of 35 times [i.e., 70%].

3. Reluctance, 'John Paul' notwithstanding, to introduce new names into the papal name pool once name change became the norm – with even 'John Paul' being a composite of two oft used names. This aspect is further discussed below.

But some 'conventions,' rather than trends *per se*, may be changing. 'John' is likely to enjoy a resurgence. The much beloved 'Good Pope' John XXIII (#262), though considered too progressive and ecumenical by conservatives, was beatified in September 2000 – 37 years after his death. He is on his way to sainthood. The veneration afforded to him should mitigate any past stigma attached to that name – in the main by the 15th century antipope John (XXIII) who earlier in his life had been a genuine seafaring pirate. Consequently, 'John' should figure among the favorites as a potential name of a future pope – especially one who has no intention of being a traditionalist or a conservative.

Though 50 years have now gone by since the last 'Pius,' it too could make a comeback – though probably never with the frequency it once enjoyed. On the other hand, it is difficult to see a pope opting for 'Clement' anytime soon. Pius XII (#261), who was pope during Word War II, though sometimes controversial, enjoys considerable respect. The day before John XIII was beatified, John Paul II (#265) bestowed the title 'venerable' on Pius XII – a formal confirmation that he is being considered for canonization. The last 'Clement,' i.e., XIV (#250), however, is unlikely to ever enjoy such reverence. He has been castigated as one of the weakest popes of all times. So, it is difficult to see a new pope wishing to be associated with him.

Following 'John Paul,' there is a distinct possibility of more two-fold names in the future – and one can only hope that a future pope does not decide to go even further and opt for a three-fold name. A two-fold name reduces the difficulty of having to make a singular hard and fast choice. It affords the option of being more magnanimous and expansive – as shown by Albino Luciani. It also provides a means of indicating balance, compromise or a theme. Thus, one could speculate on future names such as 'Pius John,' 'Leo Paul' or 'Innocent Gregory.' There is also a high probability of future 'John Pauls,' particularly so once John Paul II is beatified – as is certain to be the case.

NEW PAPAL NAMES & FREQUENCY OF USAGE

Boniface I – the halfway mark

Zosimus' (#41) turbulent and testy 21 month long papacy came to an end when he finally succumbed to a lengthy illness on December 26, 418. He had antagonized many Western clerics, and moreover had been forced to publicly recant his prior approval of Pelagianism – a heresy that disputed the significance of original sin and promoted the power of mortal will. Zosimus, believed to have been a Greek, succeeded in fissuring Church unity.

The day after Zosimus' death, the Roman deacons and a few of the presbyters barricaded themselves inside the Lateran and elected their archdeacon Eulalius as pope. Eulalius is believed to have also been Greek. His name is a Latinized version of the Greek 'Eylalios' – meaning sociable. His Greek origins, possibly coupled with his close association with Zosimus, appear to have been the rationale for his election.

The next day, December 28, the bulk of the presbyters and some laity elected Boniface. Boniface, an elderly presbyter, a son of a priest, had been a trusted emissary of Innocent I (#40) – the authoritative pope who had earned the sobriquet 'the first pope.' On December 29, both Boniface and Eulalius were consecrated at separate ceremonies – albeit with Eulalius' at the Lateran, officiated by the Bishop of Ostia [Italy], the traditional consecrator of popes.

Western Emperor Honorius (393-423), residing in Ravenna [E. Italy], was then asked to intervene. He, influenced by favorable reports from the pagan prefect of Rome, initially ruled in favor of Eulalius – the first to be elected and the one consecrated by the Bishop of Ostia. Presbyters and the Emperor's half-sister, however, objected. The Emperor summoned both contenders to a synod in Ravenna. It proved to be inconclusive.

Another synod was scheduled for June 419 in Spoleto [Italy]. Bishops from Gaul and Africa were asked to attend. Boniface and Eulalius were told to stay away from Rome until then. Eulalius, however, returned to Rome to celebrate Easter on March 30. On news of this, the Emperor banished Eulalius. On April 3, 419, 98 days after the death of Zosimus, Boniface was acknowledged as the *true* pope. The start of his papacy was backdated to his election.

Boniface did much to ameliorate the disruptions caused by Zosimus. He is said to have come up with the maxim: "It has never been lawful for what has once been decided by the apostolic see to be reconsidered." Now reduced to the more pithy: *"Roma locuta est; causa finita est"* – Rome has spoken, the cause is finished (the matter is settled).

Boniface was the 42nd pope.

Only one name had recurred to this point, viz. Xystus/Sixtus – I (7th pope) and II (24th). Thus, 'Boniface' became the 41st name to enter the papal rolls. Since there are now 81 papal names, Boniface was the halfway mark vis-à-vis papal names. Thus, within 350 years of St. Peter's martyrdom, half of the papal names had already been used – albeit with just one name being repeated.

500 to 750 – repeats start to multiply

In the next 79 years, up to November 498, there were to be eight more popes. Three of them had previously used names: viz. 'Xystus/Sixtus,' 'Felix' and 'Anastasius.' 'Anastasius' became the first name to recur within the same century, i.e., Anastasius I (#39) Nov 399 – Dec 401 and Anastasius II (#50) Nov 496 – 498. Hence this acceleration:

42 – 319: only one name, viz. 'Xystus/Sixtus,' is repeated and that just once: i.e., Xystus/Sixtus I & II.

319 – 498: three names repeated: 'Xystus/Sixtus' for the second time, 'Felix' and 'Anastasius' for the first.

'John' had yet to be used even once!

The 50 popes to hold office up to November 498 had thus used 46 names in total.

During the next 255 years, i.e., 498 – 752, there were to be 41 popes. These 41 used a total of 28 names between them – which included the first two documented name changes, i.e., John II (#56) and III (#61). 'John,' first used in 523, ended up occurring seven times. 'Boniface' occurred four times and 'Gregory' three – with Gregory I (#64), the Great, getting elected in September 590.

There were 91 popes in the 710 year period between 42 and 752. These 91 used a total of 71 names. Hence, 87% of the papal names had already occured by 752.

Only ten names would be added over the next 1,250 years. These being:

1. Paul I (#94) – 757
2. Hadrian I (#96) – 772
3. Paschal I (#99) – 817
4. Valentine (#101) -- 827
5. Nicholas I (#106) *the Great* – 858
6. Marinus I (#109) -- 882
7. Formosus (#112) – 891
8. Romanus (#115) – 897
9. Lando (#122) – 913
10. John Paul I (#264) – 1978

Name change, on a *documented basis*, only became the norm since 1009.

First to the various repetitions and the ascendancy of 'John'

Till the middle of the 6th century, 'Xystus/Sixtus,' where 'Xystus' was most likely a priestly name [p. 35], was the most repeated of the names. In 257, it became the first name to recur; 175 years later it became the first to be used thrice.

The first Boniface, as discussed above, was pope number 42 – one pope ahead of Xystus/Sixtus III (#44), who was elected in 432. Boniface II (#55) was elected 112 years after #42. But 77 years later, there was to be a spate of three popes named 'Boniface' within a 12 year span – viz. Boniface III (#66) in 607, IV (#67) in 608 and V (#69) in 619. Thanks to this spurt in usage, 'Boniface' takes the honors for being the first name to be used for the fourth time as well as for the fifth. There was a Felix IV (#54) prior to Boniface IV, but, since Felix II was an antipope, this was the third instance of a legitimate 'Felix' as opposed to the fourth.

The first pope to be named 'John' was elected by the Roman clergy on August 13, 523 – exactly a week after the death of Hormisdas (#52). John, originally from Tuscany [Italy], was an elderly and frail deacon. A schism with the East that had lasted for 35 years had been resolved four years earlier, thanks to the insistence of the new Eastern Roman Emperor Justin I (518-527). This schism had to do with the East's reluctance to accept the 451 Chalcedonian Creed, which maintained that Christ was one person with two natures, one human the other divine, united within him. The East was more partial to the monophysitic view that Christ was one person with but one nature -- the divine having subsumed the human.

Justin I, though first and foremost an ambitious politician, was devout and pro-Chalcedonian. Having ended the schism, he then set about trying to eradicate heresies -- in particular Arianism which questioned the divinity of Christ. This perturbed the Germanic Theodoric the Great the King Of Italy (493-526) -- who like many Germans of that time was an Arian. Theodoric summoned John to Ravenna and instructed him to visit Constantinople [Turkey] to change the Emperor's mind.

John, the first pope to visit the Eastern capital, was received by an unexpectedly servile and prostrative Emperor. He was asked to celebrate Easter, per the Roman rite, at the great *'Hagia Sophia,'* and given precedence over the local patriarch. The Emperor agreed to most of the King's demands bar one, which, however, was pivotal: the ability for Arians that were forced to renounce their faith to revert back to Arianism.

When John returned to Ravenna, the King was suspicious and angry. Though others were harshly punished, the King did not do bodily harm to the pope. He was just asked to remain in Ravenna while the King weighed his options. This proved too stressful for the old pope who was already drained from his arduous trip. He collapsed and died. His body was taken to Rome with much adulation. The later claims that the King threw him in prison and that he died a martyr from starvation and abuse appear to be without basis. He was buried in St. Peter's Basilica; 'victim for Christ' being his epitaph.

Mercurius and Catelinus opted for 'John,' given that John I (#52) was by then a much revered martyr. John IV (#72) was elected in 640 - 114 years after the martyrdom. Since 'John' is considered to be his birth name, there is a possibility, given the time interval, that his parents may have named him after the pope who died for Christ. The same may hold true for John V (#82) - elected in 685. Three years after his death John VI (#85) became pope. This was the first instance of six popes with the same name. This John's papacy lasted 38 months.

He was succeeded by John VII (#86) – the first instance of a name being used for the seventh time. After that, 'Johns' would become popes at a faster frequency, and more often, than those with any other name. For example, the seventh 'Boniface' was pope #194, 108 popes after John VII. The seventh 'Leo' was the closest to John VII, but even he came in at #127. Refer to Appendix C for a complete list of all the instances of the repeated papal names along with the sequence numbers to show when they occurred.

THE EBB AND FLOW IN THE POPULARITY OF 'JOHN' AS AN ASSUMED NAME

In 1003 Giovanni Fasanus chose to be John XVIII (#142) to become the 17th pope named 'John.' Of these seventeen, four are known, for a fact, to have assumed the name. The remaining thirteen are considered to have retained their prior name. After Fasanus, there would be seventeen more pope-elects whose birth names were also 'John.' None of these seventeen, however, chose to retain their birth name. They opted to be known by other names. But four other popes had no compunctions about wanting to be known as 'John.'

This split seems somewhat curious. One possible explanation could be that some of the 'Johns' felt that their name had been overused and opted to be known by other names to gain better differentiation – rather than getting lost within the plethora of prior 'Johns.' To this end, it is worth noting that by the time of the 17th 'John,' there had only been five instances of 'Gregory,' seven of 'Benedict,' eight of 'Leo' and nine of 'Stephen.' 'Clement,' 'Innocent' and 'Pius' had only occurred once. Thus, there is some merit to this hypothesis. But the fact that four others voluntarily opted to be 'Johns,' ignoring the over proliferation of the name, does, however, undermine this supposition.

The other, and probably the most likely and logical explanation, may have been the desire to uphold the tradition of name change – given the traction it was gaining. The third possibility is that the name was thought to have been tarnished – at least in the eyes of some Italians. 'Pedro' and 'Jacques' who did assume it were, respectively, Spanish and French.

John 'Octavian' XII (#131), 'the boy pope,' was elected when he was but 18 years old. His father, who had ruled Rome, had coerced the Roman leadership to ensure this outcome. John XII was noted for his rabid immorality and duplicitous politics. He did not glorify his name.

The Tusculan thread and the three-term pope

John XIX (#145), related to the voracious Tusculan family that tried to control the papacy for three decades, went from being a layman to pope in a day. Allegations of bribery swirled around him. His predecessor was his older brother Benedict VIII (#144). His successor was his 'nephew' (or possibly even son), Benedict IX (#146, #148 & #151) – who was to be pope for three turbulent terms. So these two 'Johns,' XII (#131) and XIX (#145), were certainly not exemplary. Plus, there was the inevitable machinations of Roman politics.

Just prior to his 12th anniversary as pope, Benedict IX was forced to flee Rome. The denizens were not happy with his earthly lifestyle nor the control being wielded over them by Benedict's Tusculan relatives. The competing Crescentian family then had one of their bishops, John, the Bishop of Sabina, elected as pope. He took the name Silvester III (#147) – most likely to distance himself from the Tusculan John XIX. The die was cast. A precedent set. Silvester's reign, however, lasted but 49 days.

Benedict IX soon returned to Rome with a band of followers. He ousted Silvester and started his second term as pope. But he soon lost interest. The story is that he was eager to be wealthy and wed. So he handed over his papacy to his godfather, John Gratian, the elderly archpriest at Rome's *San Giovanni a Porta Latina*, in exchange for a large sum of money. Some even claim that the amount involved was 1,450 pounds of gold.

It is said that those present when John took office urged him to assume the name 'Gregory,' in the hopes that he would emulate 'the Great' (#64). He thus became Gregory VI (#149). It is possible that he did want to change his name anyway, and made sure that it appeared that he did so due to public acclamation. Not being known as 'John' would enable him to downplay his Tusculan associations. It would distance him from the Tusculan John XIX who had only been dead for 13 years. The bottom line here, however, is that two successive 'Johns' had opted to surrender their birth name. It was becoming a fad.

The next 'Giovanni,' viz. Giovanni Coniulo, 72 years and 12 popes later, opted to be Gelasius II (#162) – the only instance of this illustrious papal name being assumed. Gelasius I (#49) was exceptionally astute. He articulated the *Duo sunt* (two sword) notion of asymmetrical power sharing between royals and the pope. It was he who also co-opted the incisive

'Vicar of Christ' title. Coniulo was elected towards the end of a particularly tumultuous period that had seen at least three antipopes and considerable royal interference. Hence, he may have chosen his regnal name to remind royals that in the end the pope's priestly powers trumped those wielded by royals – since popes would determine the fate of royals come the day of judgment. After Coniulo it was now 3-for-3 when it came to 'Johns' assuming a new name upon becoming pope.

The two non-Italian 'Johns'

After the Tusculan John XIX (#145), it would take 244 years and 42 intervening popes (counting Benedict IX but once) before there was to be another pope named 'John.' In September 1276, Pedro Julião was elected pope. He was to be the third pope elected that year and the fourth person to hold that office during that eventful year. Prior to being elected, he had been the Cardinal Bishop of Tusculum [15 miles SE Rome] – Tusculum, from the 10th to the 12th century, having been the 'fiefdom' of the Tusculan family.

Pedro was born in Portugal. He was a physician as was his father. Blessed Gregory X (#185), the ex-crusader, relied on Pedro for all of his medical care. The oft made claim that Pedro was the only Portuguese pope and the only physician to be a pope might, however, be an overstatement. St. Damasus I (#37) is believed to have been born in Guimarães, Portugal while Paul IV's (#224) maternal grandmother was a Portuguese noblewoman. St. Eusebius (#31), a Greek, is believed to have been a physician. As with Pedro, he, too, might have been the son of a physician.

Pedro was noted for his scholarship that encompassed medicine, theology, physics, logic and philosophy. He had written an acclaimed text book on logic (*Summulæ logicales*), a handbook on medicinal remedies (*Thesaurus Pauperum*), a guide for treating eye diseases (*De Oculis*) and a treatise on psychology (*Scientia Libri de Anima*), which included a chapter on the workings of the heart. Given these credentials and his exposure to the papal court as Gregory's physician, he is unlikely to have been capricious in deciding to be known as John XXI (#188).

There is a likelihood that he may have chosen it in part to reflect his tenure in Tusculum. He may have also felt that this historic name needed to be revived. He also specified the 'XXI' numbering. The last 'John,' whether it be as pope or antipope, had been the Tusculan XIX (#145).

With his background in logic, he was, no doubt, trying to correct the numbering sequence associated with his name, which appears to have been in disarray since John XV (#138). The issues related to the numbering of the 'Johns' is discussed in detail starting on page 82.

John XXI's papacy came to an unexpected and unfortunate end eight months into his papacy. The ceiling of a study that had been hastily constructed for him at the papal palace in Viterbo [60 miles N of Rome] collapsed on top of him. He was fatally injured. There would be a 39 year, eight pope gap before the next 'John.' That was to be the Frenchman Jacques Duèze, Cardinal Bishop of Porto [Portugal]. He chose to be John XXII (#197). Given his ties to Portugal, he may have chosen that name to honor the Portuguese John XXI.

Three competing popes

During 1309 to 1377, the papacy was based in Avignon [SE France] rather than in Rome. This involved seven successive popes, all French, the second of whom was John XXII (#197). The last of the seven was Gregory XI (#202). He would be the last, to-date, of the total of sixteen French popes. In October 1376, urged by the Romans and hoping to quell unrest in the Papal States, Gregory elected to move the papacy back to Rome. He arrived in Rome in January 1377, after a grueling two month sea voyage.

Gregory XI died in March 1378 from complications caused by bladder stones. Pressured by rioting Romans, 16 cardinals quickly elected the Italian Bartolomeo Prigano, Archbishop of Bari [Italy] – who became Urban VI (#203). Six months later, the cardinals, most of whom were French, started to regret their rushed selection. So, they decided to appoint a competing pope – viz. Clement (VII). The Great Western Schism, which was to last from 1378 to 1417, had begun. Between October 1378 and June 1409, there would be two sets of rival popes: one set residing in Rome and the other in Avignon as follows:

ROME	AVIGNON
Urban VI (#203), Italian, 1378-1389	Clement (VII), French/Italian, 1378-1394
Boniface IX (#204), Italian, 1389-1404	
	Benedict (XIII), 'Spanish,' 1394-1417
Innocent VII (#205), Italian, 1404-1406	
Gregory XII (#206), Italian, 1406-1415	

Into this fray now entered the Neapolitan Baldassare Cossa - a genuine buccaneer and an unabashed philanderer. He had been a pirate in his youth. He then went to Bologna [Italy] and earned a degree in law. He was made Archdeacon of Bologna by Boniface IX - also a Neapolitan. He would soon be the papal treasurer and a cardinal. He had won the pope's gratitude by helping out on military matters involving the Papal States. He amassed considerable wealth and power thanks to these new responsibilities. He was, nonetheless, anxious to see an end to the schism - maybe to gain access to more assets and power.

He started to conspire with other cardinals in Rome and in Avignon. Then, using the resources at his disposal, he convened a council of cardinals in Pisa [Italy] in March of 1409. This council deposed both Gregory and Benedict. On June 26, 1409, the cardinals elected Cardinal Pietro Philarghi, a Cretan, as pope. He opted to be Alexander (V). Rather than putting an end to the schism, they had succeeded in creating yet another rival pope. Alexander's reign, big on promises, light on results and marked with largess to a select few, was to last but 10 months.

He was manipulated throughout by Baldassare and died, suspiciously, while in his company in Bologna. These suspicions did not, however, preclude the cardinals from the Pisa council, now gathered in Bologna, from electing Baldassare as Alexander's successor. Bribery, coercion and pressure from the King of Naples appear to have played a large role in this election. Baldassare chose to be John (XXIII) - probably because John XXII (#197) had had close ties with Naples.

In 1414, John XXIII, at the behest of his new ally the German King Sigismund (1410-1437), convened the Council of Constance [Germany] with the express purpose of ending the schism. In 1415, he, to his consternation and cost, was, however, the first to be deposed by this council, rather than one of the other two popes: i.e., Gregory XII and Benedict (XIII).

Though accused of multiple sins, mainly to do with earthly pleasures, he was not explicitly deemed an antipope *per se* at this juncture since many at the council believed in the legitimacy of the Pisan councils. Following his colorful exploits, there was not to be another 'John,' pope or antipope, for another 543 years - the longest gap, by far.

Il Papa Buono – the good pope John

On October 28, 1958, three days into the conclave that followed the death of Pius XII (#261), Cardinal Angelo Giuseppe Roncalli, Patriarch of Venice, was elected pope. He was a month shy of his 77th birthday. He had attended a seminary at eleven and was ordained a priest in 1904 when 23. During WW I, having been drafted as a sergeant, he served in the Italian Army's medical corps as an orderly before being made a chaplain in 1916.

In 1925, Pius XI (#260) made him a bishop and set him forth as a diplomat for the Holy See. For the next 19 years, he self-effacingly served Rome with rare distinction in Bulgaria, Turkey and Greece. During WW II he indefatigably aided Jewish families seeking refuge. In 1944 Pius XII made him the Apostolic Nuncio to Paris – a pivotal post during those troubled times.

Prior to the conclave, Angelo Giuseppe did not presume he would be pope, though bookmakers had him ahead of the other *papabili* at 2-1. He was noted for his humility and was also very familiar with the invariably true adage: *"whoever goes into the conclave as pope exits as cardinal."* It is said that he left Venice with a return train ticket and is known to have told folks he met in Rome that he would meet with them back in Venice.

But by the second night of the conclave, he and his supporters knew that he would get the necessary votes to be elected pope. He thus had time to think about the name he would choose. Given the immense esteem he was held in by all who knew him, he did not have to worry about how a name would reflect upon him. He had the standing to select any name that he wanted. And that is exactly what he did.

When asked by Cardinal Tisserant, the Dean of the College of Cardinals, as to what name he wished to be called he firmly stated: *"Vocabor Johannes"* (I will be called John). He then produced some notes and explained his choice. His full, humor laced, explanation can be found in chapter 6. But his key rationale was that his father was named 'John.' He also stated that there had been 22 legitimate popes named 'John' – thereby intimating that Baldassare Cossa was an antipope. Later he confirmed Baldassare's antipope status by declaring that he would indeed be John XXIII (#262) – rather than XXIV.

TRENDS IN PAPAL NAMES BY 250 YEAR BLOCKS

TIME PERIOD	250 YEAR BLOCKS	500 YEAR BLOCKS	1,000 YEAR BLOCKS
1st '250' years c. 42 – 250 [209 years] popes: #1 - #20	20 popes 20 names [1:1 ratio] *0 name changes* *no name was repeated*	50 popes 46 names [1.09:1 ratio] *0 name changes* MOST PREVALENT: Sixtus x3 Anastasius x2 Felix x2	
2nd '250' years 251 – 498 [248 years] popes: #21 - #50	30 popes 27 names [1.11:1 ratio] *0 name changes* MOST PREVALENT: Anastasius x2 Felix x2 Sixtus x2		139 popes 80 names [1.74:1 ratio] 5 name changes [3.6%] MOST PREVALENT: John x15 Stephen x9 Leo x8
3rd '250' years 498 – 752 [255 years] popes: #51 - #91	41 popes 28 names [1.46:1 ratio] 2 name changes [5%] MOST PREVALENT: John x7 Boniface x4 Gregory x3	89 popes 39 names [2.28:1 ratio] 5 name changes [5.6%] MOST PREVALENT: John x15 Stephen x8 Benedict x7 Leo x7	
4th '250' years 752 – 999 [248 years] popes: #92 - #139	48 popes 20 names [2.4:1 ratio] 3 name changes [6.25%] MOST PREVALENT: John x8 Stephen x8 Leo x6		

TIME PERIOD	250 YEAR BLOCKS	500 YEAR BLOCKS	1,000 YEAR BLOCKS
5th '250' years 999 – 1254 [256 years] popes: #140 - #181	42 popes* 23 names [1.82:1 ratio] 38 name changes [90.5%] MOST PREVALENT: Gregory x4 Celestine x3 Innocent x3 John x3	76 popes* 28 names [2.71:1 ratio] 72 name changes [94.7%]	
6th '250' years 1254 – 1503 [250 years] popes: #182 - #215	34 popes 18 names [1.88:1 ratio] 34 name changes [100%] MOST PREVALENT: Innocent x4 Clement, Gregory, Nicholas & Urban x3 each	MOST PREVALENT: Gregory x7 Innocent x7 Clement x5 John x5 Urban x5	126 popes* 31 names [4.06:1 ratio] 119 name changes [94.4%]
7th '250' years 1503 – 1758 [256 years] popes: #216 - #248	33 popes 13 names [2.54:1 ratio] 30 name changes [91%] MOST PREVALENT: Clement x6 Innocent x5 Gregory, Paul & Pius x3 each	50 popes 15 names [3.33:1 ratio] 47 name changes [94%]	MOST PREVALENT: Clement x13, Innocent x12 Gregory x11 Pius x11 Benedict x7
8th '250' years 1758 – 2005 [248 years] popes: #249 - #265	17 popes 8 names [2.13:1 ratio] 17 name changes [100%] MOST PREVALENT: Pius x7 Clement, John Paul & Leo x2 each	MOST PREVALENT: Pius x10 Clement x8 Innocent x5	* Counting Benedict IX's 3 terms as separate but only counting the name change once.

TIME PERIOD	CURRENT		
9th '250' years 2005 – popes: #266 –	1 pope 1 name [1:1 ratio] 1 name change [100%]		

	FIRST 2,000 YEARS	IN TOTAL TO-DATE
POPES [WITH BENEDICT IX'S 3 TERMS]	265	266
NAMES	81 [~ratio 3.27:1]	
NAME CHANGES [COUNTING BENEDICT IX JUST ONCE]	124 [46.8%]	125 [47%]
MOST PREVALENT	John　　x21 Gregory　x16 Benedict　x14 Clement　x14	John　　x21 Gregory　x16 Benedict　x15 Clement　x14

TRENDS IN PAPAL NAMES BY CENTURY

'CENTURY'	POPES	NAMES	NAME CHANGES	MOST PREVALENT
'1st' 60 years c. 42 – c.101	4 #1 - #4	4 1:1	0	
'2nd' 99 years 101 – 199	10 #5 - #14	10 1:1	0	
'3rd' 106 years 199 – 304	15 #15 - #29	15 1:1	0	

'Century'	Popes	Names	Name Changes	Most Prevalent	
'4th' 94 years 306 – 399	9 #30 - #38	9 1:1	0		
'5th' 100 years 399 – 498	12 #39 - #50	11 1.1:1	0	Anastasius	x2
'6th' 107 years 498 – 604	14 #51 - #64	10 1.4:1	2 14.3%	John Benedict Pelagius	x3 x2 x2
'7th' 98 years 604 – 701	20 #65 - #84	17 1.2:1	0	Boniface John	x3 x2
'8th' 95 years 701 – 795	12 #85 - #96	8 1.5:1	0	Stephen Gregory John	x3 x2 x2
'9th' 106 years 795 – 900	21 #97 - #117	16 1.3:1	0	Stephen Hadrian John Leo	x3 x2 x2 x2
'10th' 100 years 900 – 999	22 #118 - #139	10 2.2:1	3 13.6%	John Benedict Leo	x6 x4 x4
'11th' 101 years 999 – 1099	21* #140 - #160	13 1.6:1	17* 81%	John Benedict Gregory Silvester Victor	x3 x2 x2 x2 x2
'12th' 100 years 1099 – 1198	16 #161 - #176	14 1.14:1	16 100%	Celestine Lucius	x2 x2
'13th' 106 years 1198 – 1303	18 #177 - #194	12 1.5:1	18 100%	Innocent Celestine Gregory Honorius Nicholas	x3 x2 x2 x2 x2
'14th' 102 years 1303 – 1404	10 #195 - #204	7 1.43:1	10 100%	Benedict Clement Urban	x2 x2 x2

* The '11th' century includes the 3 terms of Benedict IX counted as separate instances – though the name change and the name is only counted but once.

'Century'	Popes	Names	Name Changes	Most Prevalent	
'15th' 100 years 1404 – 1503	11 #205 - #215	10 1.1:1	11 100%	Innocent	x2
'16th' 103 years 1503 – 1605	17 #216 - #232	11 1.54:1	14 82%	Pius Clement Gregory Julius Paul	x3 x2 x2 x2 x2
'17th' 96 years 1605 – 1700	11 #233 - #243	7 1.57:1	11 100%	Innocent Alexander Clement	x3 x2 x2
'18th' 100 years 1700 – 1799	8 #244 - #251	4 2:1	8 100%	Clement Benedict	x4 x2
'19th' 104 years 1800 – 1903	6 #252 - #257	3 2:1	6 100%	Pius Leo	x3 x2
'20th' 103 years 1903 – 2005	8 #258 - #265	5 1.6:1	8 100%	Pius John Paul	x3 x2
'21st' 2005 –	1 so far #266 -	1 so far 1:1	1 so far 100%		

Figure 18: The 2.6 acre Palais des Papes at Avignon, France. Benedict XII (#198) started having it built on top of the bishop's residence in the 1330s. Work on it continued under the other Avignon popes until 1364.

IV:
THE NAMES

 he papal roll per Appendix B contains 81 elemental [i.e., uncompounded] papal names. 45 of these, starting with Peter (#1) and ending with Lando (#122), have only occurred once. The other 36 have recurred at least twice; ten of these, 'John Paul' being the latest, occurring but twice. These 36 repeated names are distributed across 221 popes, 30 of them serving as the source pool for the assumed papal names. The diagram below quantifies the relationships between the 266 popes and the 81 elemental names used by them.

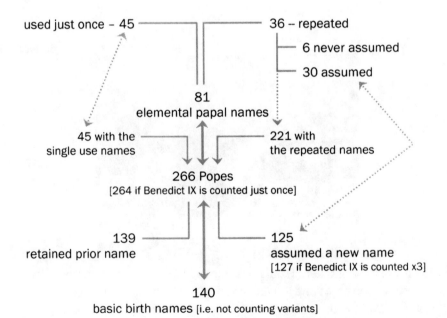

used just once – 45 ——————————— 36 -- repeated

├— 6 never assumed

└— 30 assumed

81
elemental papal names

45 with the ——————— 221 with
single use names   the repeated names

266 Popes
[264 if Benedict IX is counted just once]

139 ————— 125
retained prior name   assumed a new name
[127 if Benedict IX is counted x3]

140
basic birth names [i.e. not counting variants]

The 45 names that have only occurred once were, without exception, prior names that were retained – whether they were birth or priestly.

At present, there is no singular instance of an assumed name. With the exception of 'John Paul,' all 29 of the other assumed names had originally been the birth or priestly name of an earlier pope. That means that there had always been a prior occurrence before a name was assumed. In other words, 'John Paul' has been the only innovation vis-à-vis assumed names. But it was reused within 51 days. It thus lost its short-lived distinction of having been the only assumed name that had stood alone within the papal roll.

The above distinction should not, however, be confused with names that have been assumed but once. There are seven such names: viz. Anastasius, Damasus, Gelasius, Julius, Paschal, Sergius and Stephen. Of these, 'Stephen' is the most noteworthy. There have been 10 'Stephens' – albeit counting the original Stephen II (#92), whose papacy lasted just four days. But there has only been one instance of this auspicious name, that of the Christian Protomartyr, being assumed. That was in 1057. Frederick of Lorraine [France], Abbot of Monte Cassino [Italy], opted to be Stephen IX (#155) because he was elected on August 2 – St. Stephen I's (#23) feast day.

Though his reign was short, this Stephen, pious and forthright, did not in anyway sully the name. So he *per se* cannot be held accountable for the apparent sidelining of this name since his pontificate. The culprit, however, may have been Stephen VI (#114), the instigator of the infamous Cadaver Synod [p. 10], who became so unpopular that he was eventually strangled to death.

The rather brief pontificates associated with this name may be another factor. The average reign for the ten 'Stephens' is 2.6 years – way below the 7 year average for the entire population of popes. In 1958, Angelo Roncalli ended his explanation as to why he chose to be John XXIII (#262) [p. 62 & 96] by quipping that nearly all the popes named 'John' have had brief pontificates. But, in reality, the average for the 'Johns' is nearly twice as long as that for the 'Stephens.' So the possibility of unusual brevity may be the real rub as to the reluctance to assume 'Stephen.'

The list of 81
The 81 elemental papal names are listed below, in chronological order of appearance, along with when each name was used for the first and last

time. How many times each occurred and was assumed is also shown – along with the 'assumed quotient' [i.e., assumed/used x 100.] Refer to Appendix B for more precise dates. Breaks in succession indicating the appearance of prior names are highlighted by an underline in the 'FIRST' column. Appendix C provides another perspective.

	NAME	USED	ASSUMED	FIRST	LAST
1	Peter	1		#1, c. 42	
2	Linus	1		#2, c. 64	
3	Anacletus	1		#3, c. 76	
4	Clement	14	13 (93%)	#4, c. 88	#250, 1769
5	Evaristus	1		#5, c. 97	
6	Alexander	7	6 (86%)	#6, c. 105	#242, 1689
7	Sixtus	5	2 (40%)	#7, c. 115	#228, 1585
8	Telesphorus	1		#8, c. 125	
9	Hyginus	1		#9, c. 136	
10	Pius	12	11 (92%)	#10, c. 140	#261, 1939
11	Anicetus	1		#11, c. 154	
12	Soter	1		#12, c. 166	
13	Eleutherius	1		#13, c. 174	
14	Victor	3	2 (67%)	#14, 189	#159, 1087
15	Zephyrinus	1		#15, 199	
16	Callistus	3	2 (67%)	#16, 217	#210, 1455
17	Urban	8	2 (88%)	#17, 222	#236, 1623
18	Pontian	1		#18, 230	
19	Anterus	1		#19, 235	
20	Fabian	1		#20, 236	
21	Cornelius	1		#21, 251	
22	Lucius	3	2 (67%)	#22, 253	#172, 1181
23	Stephen	10	1 (10%)	#23, 254	#155, 1057
24	Dionysius	1		#25, 260	
25	Felix	3	0 (0%)	#26, 269	#54, 526
26	Eutychian	1		#27, 275	

	Name	Used	Assumed	First	Last
27	Caius	1		#28, 283	
28	Marcellinus	1		#29, 296	
29	Marcellus	2	0 (0%)	#30, 306	#223, 1555
30	Eusebius	1		#31, 308	
31	Miltiades	1		#32, 311	
32	Silvester	3	2 (67%)	#33, 314	#147, 1045
33	Mark	1		#34, 336	
34	Julius	3	1 (34%)	#35, 337	#222, 1550
35	Liberius	1		#36, 352	
36	Damasus	2	1 (50%)	#37, 366	#152, 1048
37	Siricius	1		#38, 384	
38	Anastasius	4	1 (25%)	#39, 399	#169, 1153
39	Innocent	13	12 (92%)	#40, 401	#245, 1721
40	Zosimus	1		#41, 417	
41	Boniface	8	2 (25%)	#42, 418	#204, 1389
42	Celestine	5	4 (80%)	#43, 422	#193, 1294
43	Leo	13	5 (39%)	#45, 440	#257, 1878
44	Hilarius	1		#46, 461	
45	Simplicius	1		#47, 468	
46	Gelasius	2	1 (50%)	#49, 492	#162, 1118
47	Symmachus	1		#51, 498	
48	Hormisdas	1		#52, 514	
49	John	21	8 (38%)	#53, 523	#262, 1958
50	Agapetus	2	0 (0%)	#57, 535	#130, 946
51	Silverius	1		#58, 536	
52	Vigilius	1		#59, 537	
53	Pelagius	2	0 (0%)	#60, 556	#63, 579
54	Benedict *[IX just once]*	15	8 (53%)	#62, 575	#266, 2005

	Name	Used	Assumed	First	Last
55	Gregory	16	12 (75%)	#64, 590	#255, 1831
56	Sabinian	1		#65, 604	
57	Deusdedit	1		#68, 615	
58	Honorius	4	3 (75%)	#70, 625	#191, 1285
59	Severinus	1		#71, 640	
60	Theodore	2	0 (0%)	#73, 642	#116, 897
61	Martin	3	2 (67%)	#74, 649	#207, 1417
62	Eugene	4	2 (50%)	#75, 654	#208, 1431
63	Vitalian	1		#76, 657	
64	Adeodatus	1		#77, 672	
65	Donus	1		#78, 676	
66	Agatho	1		#79, 678	
67	Conon	1		#83, 686	
68	Sergius	4	1 (25%)	#84, 687	#143, 1009
69	Sisinnius	1		#87, 708	
70	Constantine	1		#88, 708	
71	Zacharias	1		#91, 741	
72	Paul	6	5 (83%)	#94, 757	#263, 1963
73	Hadrian	6	2 (33%)	#96, 772	#219, 1522
74	Paschal	2	1 (50%)	#99, 817	#161, 1099
75	Valentine	1		#101, 827	
76	Nicholas	5	4 (80%)	#106, 858	#209, 1447
77	Marinus	2	0 (0%)	#109, 882	#129, 942
78	Formosus	1		#112, 891	
79	Romanus	1		#115, 897	
80	Lando	1		#122, 913	
81	John Paul	2	2 (100%)	#264, 1978	#265, 1978

The compactness of the above list can be exploited to gain visual confirmation of the following:

    Name repetition, indicated by the underscored breaks in the sequence numbers, was rare and sporadic until the 6th century – as discussed in the previous chapter.

    The marked paucity of acclaimed biblical names, in particular those of the Apostles. The first 'Paul' to be elected was in 757 while the first 'John' was in 523. There has yet to be a pope named 'Andrew,' 'James,' 'Matthew,' 'Philip,' 'Thomas' or 'Simon.' There have been fives popes whose birth names were 'Jacob' – a variant of 'James.' But all five opted to assume other names such as 'Benedict' (#198) and 'John' (#197). Maffeo Barberini, if he had opted to retain his birth name, could have become the first 'Matthew.' Instead, he chose to be Urban VIII (#236). The only 'Simon' to-date became Martin IV (#190), possibly to avoid being 'Peter II' in a roundabout way, while Nicholas V (#209) was the only 'Thomas.'

    The august name 'Constantine' only appears once, and that nearly 400 years after the reign of the bestriding emperor. Its association with Rome's nemesis, Constantinople, probably explains why this name has never been assumed.

    'Clement' (x13), 'Innocent' (x12), 'Gregory' (x12) and 'Pius' (x11) are the most widely assumed of the names – with 'Clement,' 'Innocent' and 'Pius' only having occurred once each as a birth or priestly name.

    'Eugene' followed 'Martin' on their first appearance [i.e., #74 & #75] as well as their last [i.e., #207 & #208].

RECURRENCE FACTORS, DURABILITY AND POPULARITY

'John Paul' is the only instance when the first two occurrences of a name were consecutive: i.e., #264 and #265. In the case of the other 35 repeated names, there are on average 81 intervening papacies between the first and second occurrence of a papal name. For sixteen of the names [i.e., 44%], the gap between 'I' and 'II' is in excess of 100 with 'Pius' setting the record with 200.

Figure 19: Enea Piccolomini, 'Cardinal of Siena,' when elected by acclamation in August 1458, chose to be Pius II (#211). Scholarly, published, and once a rather worldly poet laureate, he chose that name because the protagonist in Virgil's (29-19 BC) epic poem *Aeneid* describes himself as *pius Aeneas* – 'Aeneas' being the Latin form of his first name. The prior 'Pius' (#10), believed to have been the first sole Bishop of Rome, had reigned 1,300 years and 200 popes earlier. This is the longest gap between the first and second instance of a papal name. Image by Pinturicchio (15th cent.).

The six shortest and longest gaps between 'I' and 'II' are:

1. John Paul #264 & #265   [0 intervening papacies, 51 days]

2. John #53 & #56   [2 intervening, 9 years 4 months]

3. Pelagius #60 & #63   [2 intervening, 23 years ~4 months]

4. Hadrian #96 & #107   [10 intervening, ~96 years]

5. Anastasius #39 & #50   [10 intervening, 97 years]

6. Boniface #42 & #55   [12 intervening, 111 years 9 months]

ಛ ಛ ಛ ಛ

6. Clement #4 & #150   [145 intervening papacies, ~956 years]

5. Callistus #16 & #163   [146 intervening, ~902 years]

4. Alexander #157 & #6   [150 intervening, ~955 years]

3. Julius #35 & #217   [181 intervening, ~1,166 years]

2. Marcellus #30 & #223   [192 intervening, ~1,248 years]

1. Pius #10 & #211   [200 intervening, ~1,317 years]

Once it was reintroduced, 'Pius' became the most popular of the names – being assumed ten times over the next 500 years, with three instances of consecutive usage: i.e., #225/#226, #251/#252 & #260/#261.

During the last 500 years, 'Pius,' on average, was assumed by every 5th pope.

Recurrence factors

The notion of how often a name was repeated, as with the ten instances of 'Pius' above, can be generalized and represented by a 'recurrence factor.' The four instances of popes named 'Sergius,' i.e., #84, #103, #120 and #143, can be used to quickly demonstrate how this 'recurrence factor' is calculated. The number of intervening papacies between the four instances are 18 (i.e., #103 - #84), 16 and 22. The rounded up average of these three numbers, 19 (i.e., 56÷3), is the 'recurrence factor.' It denotes that during the span of time when 'Sergius' was in use it would recur, *on average*, after a gap of 19 other papacies.

The recurrence factor provides a consistent metric by which to compare the relative rate of reappearance of the 36 repeated names. Of the widely used names, 'John' has the shortest recurrence factor – viz. 9. Given the gap of 64 papacies prior to John XXIII (#262), this number may appear, at first blush, to be too small. 'John,' however, with three instances of consecutive usage and seven instances of two papacy gaps occurred in tight clusters up to the 12th century. Its recurrence factor during that era was an impressive 4. It is the 42 papacy gap between XIX (#145) and XXI (#188) and the 62 papacy gap between XXII (#197) and XXIII (#262) that more than doubled this number.

Figure 20: The cathedral (*Duomo*) in Pienza [Tuscany, Italy – 20 SE of Siena]. Pienza was built at Pope Pius II's (#211) behest as a model Renaissance community atop what was the village of Corsignano – his birthplace. Pius named it 'Pienza' to reflect his papal name. His summer residence there is named 'Palazzo Piccolomini' per his family name. Pienza was designated a World Heritage Site by UNESCO in 1996.

Only 'Pelagius' (viz. 2) and 'John Paul' (viz. 0) have shorter recurrence factors than 'John.' But since both of these names have only occurred twice, their recurrence factors are skewed and unrepresentative. The same holds true for the three names with the longest recurrence factors: viz. Marcellus (192), Damasus (114) and Gelasius (112). All three have occurred but twice. 'Gregory' and 'Benedict' *(albeit counting IX thrice)*, each with a factor of 12, come immediately below 'John.' Thus, the three most prevalent of the elemental papal names have, as is to be hoped, relatively short recurrence factors.

The 'recurrence factors' for the nine most prevalent names, in ascending order of the 'recurrence factor,' are as follows (with the number in parenthesis showing the total instances of usage of that name):

1. John (x21) – 9
2. Benedict (x17) – 12
3. Gregory (x16) – 12
4. Stephen (x10) – 14
5. Innocent (x13) – 16
6. Leo (x13) – 17
7. Clement (x14) – 18
8. Pius (x12) – 22
9. Boniface (x8) – 22

'Felix,' that occurred thrice relatively quickly and thereby earned a recurrence factor of 13, is the only name that splits up the nine names above. 'Urban,' which, like 'Boniface,' occurred eight times, has a recurrence factor of 30, while that for 'Paul' is 33, 'Nicholas' is 25 and 'Celestine' is 37.

The durability factor

The recurrence factor denotes the rate at which names reappeared. Durability, on the other hand, gauges the longevity, or staying power, of a repeated name. It is a measure of the span of a name between its first and last occurrence. Lets take the two instances of 'Pelagius' – I (#60) and II (#63). It spanned four papacies over a 63 year period. It has the shortest span next to 'John Paul.' 'Benedict,' in contrast, now has a span encompassing 205 papacies spread over 1,430 years. It has thus proved to be a rather durable name – but by no means the most durable. In reality it is, at present, but the ninth most durable name.

The ten most durable names in terms of papacies encompassed, in descending order, are as follows with their respective spans shown both in terms of papacies and number of years:

1. Pius 252 papacies, 1,799 years
2. Clement 247, 1,681
3. Alexander 237, 1,584
4. Sixtus 222, 1,470

5. Urban 220, *1,401*

6. Leo 213, 1,438

7. John 210, 1,435

8. Innocent 206, *1,320*

9. Benedict 205, 1,430

10. Callistus 195, 1,238

Note that, if durability is ranked by the years spanned, the rankings will differ after the first four with the longest spans, i.e., the 1,401 years for 'Urban' would come in 8th as opposed to 5th. Also, 'Marcellus' with 1,249 (194 papacies) and 'Gregory' with 1,241 (192 papacies) would usurp 'Callistus.' However, ranking durability in terms of papacies spanned seems fairer since it eliminates discrepancies caused by lengthy interregnums and papacies cut short by external interference.

Whereas the most prevalent of the names all had short recurrence factors, the correlation is not as strong when it comes to durability. Only six of the top ten most prevalent names appear in the above list of the most durable – and even those not in order of their numerousness: e.g., Pius (x12) and Leo (x13) come ahead of John (x21) and Benedict (x15). This is to be expected since durability is purely a measure of the span [i.e., distance] between the first and last instance of a name. The number of times a name has been used has no bearing on its durability.

Popularity of the names – overall and assumed
Once the durability spans have been determined, it is but a logical and easy step to calculate a meaningful relative popularity quotient for the repeated names. Take 'Benedict,' which has a durability that spans 205 papacies. Seventeen of these 205 popes were named 'Benedict' *(counting IX thrice)* giving that name an overall popularity quotient of 8% [i.e., 17÷205x100]. Ten of those fifteen assumed the name 'Benedict.' This gives it an assumed name popularity quotient of 5% [i.e., 10÷205x100].

The overall and assumed popularity quotients for the ten most prevalent names, in descending order of prevalency, are:

1. John (x21): 10% overall, 4% assumed

2. Benedict *(x17)*: 8%, 5%

3. Gregory (x16): 8%, 6%

4. Clement (x16): 6%, 5%

5. Innocent (x13): 6%, 6%

6. Leo (x13): 6%, 2%

7. Pius (x12): 5%, 4%

8. Stephen (x10): 8%, 1%

9. Boniface (x8): 5%, 1%

10. Urban (x8): 4%, 1%

There is, as is to be expected, a correlation between prevalency and the overall popularity quotient – albeit with 'Stephen' demonstrating that there can be exceptions. The assumed quotient is more telling with 'Gregory,' 'Innocent' and 'Clement' taking precedence over the others (with that for 'Benedict' skewed by the three instances of IX). While the depressed assumed quotient for 'Leo' could increase in time, the chances of 'Stephen,' 'Boniface' or 'Urban' being assumed are considerably lower.

The last 'Leo,' i.e., Leo XIII (#257), though a tad conservative and cavalier in his assessment of non-Catholics, did much to enhance the prestige afforded to the papacy. Having been elected in 1878, he is credited, rightly, with ushering the Catholic church into the modern age. He lived to be 93 and enjoyed the third longest papacy to date: 25 years and 5 months. He holds the distinction of being the first pope to be filmed and also have his voice recorded. Thus, this august name, that of the first 'Great' and the one borne by the most number of canonized popes, is unsullied and primed for reuse.

REVERENCE AND DURATION OF REIGNS

The current papal roll contains 78 canonized popes (as listed in Appendix A). These canonizations, however, were chronologically front loaded: 49 of the first 50 popes and 70 of the first 100 popes are saints. There have only been five popes canonized since 885 (#110 onwards) – these being Leo IX (#153), Gregory VII (#158), Celestine (#193), Pius V (#226) and Pius X (#258). Consequently, when it comes to canonizations, the older papal names are invariably better represented.

There are only seven instances of canonized popes that share the same elemental name. These being:

1. Leo: x5
2. Gregory: x4
3. Felix: x3
4. Pius: x3
5. Xystus/Sixtus: x3
6. Boniface: x2
7. Celestine: x2

Hence, the canonization rates for the nine most prevalent names are:

1. John (x21): 5%
2. Gregory (x16): 25%
3. Benedict (x15): 7%
4. Clement (x14): 7%
5. Innocent (x13): 8%
6. Leo (x13): 39%
7. Pius (x12): 25%
8. Stephen (x10): 10%
9. Boniface (x8): 25%

The rates for the other three names, not in the above list, are: Felix (x3): 100%, Sixtus (x5): 60% and Celestine (x5): 40% – with 'Felix' and 'Sixtus' benefiting from their early popularity. The low canonization rates for popes named 'Benedict,' 'Clement' and 'Innocent' can be explained in part by the sharp drop off in papal canonizations as of the 9th century – St. Hadrian III (#110) being the 'cut-off' point, so to speak. All of the non-canonized 'Clements' and 'Innocents' came after this 'cut-off' point as did twelve of the 'Benedicts' – though it is safe to say that Benedict IX (#146, #148 & #151) is unlikely to be canonized anytime soon.

That only one of the 21 popes named 'John' have been canonized, to date, does beg some scrutiny – especially since there had been six, i.e., II (#56) to VIII (#108), prior to the 'cut-off.' John II is the 4th 'oldest' [i.e., earliest] pope not to be canonized – with Liberius (#36), who reneged on his stance on Arianism [p. 46], being the 'oldest.' John III (#61) is the 7th 'oldest' while John IV (#72) is the 15th.

John II set a bad precedent by blatantly contradicting a prior pope, i.e., Hormisdas (#52), on Christology, to curry favor with the Eastern Emperor. Subsequent popes appear, understandably, to have held this against him. John III's downfall was the Lombard invasion of Italy. He prevailed upon the Imperial 'viceroy,' the disliked and elderly Narses, then resident in Naples, to come and defend Rome. Though Narses was successful in this, he proved to be disruptive and divisive. To escape the ire of the Romans, John vacated the city and tried to conduct his duties from a rural church outside Rome.

There appears to have been nothing amiss with John IV's papacy. He was forthright, charitable and placating. But his reign lasted but 22 months. This may have been the primary reason for him being overlooked – at a juncture when papal canonizations were ceasing to be rote. With John XXIII (#262) now beatified, it is fairly certain that there will be a second Pope St. John sometime in the future – hopefully without too much delay.

At present, in addition to John XXIII, there are nine other popes who have been beatified. These being, in chronological order of their papacies: Victor III (#159), Urban II (#160), Eugene III (#168), Gregory X (#185), Innocent V (#186), Benedict XI (#195), Urban V (#201), Innocent XI (#214) and Pius IX (#256).

Duration of reigns

One other metric of interest when it comes to the 36 repeated papal names is the durations of the respective pontificates on a per elemental name basis. For example, the sixteen popes named 'Gregory' reigned, in total, for over 138 years, with an average pontificate duration of 8.65 years – with Gregory IV's (#102) being the longest at ~16 years and Gregory VIII's (#174) the shortest at 57 days.

The 265 popes prior to Benedict XVI (#266) are believed to have reigned, in total, for about 1,906 years – with the dates, in particular for the early popes, being approximations at best. If St. Peter's (#1) ministry in Rome is thought to have started c. 42, the duration between then and John Paul II's (#265) death in 2005 is 1,963 years.

Interregnums, such as the at least 3 year long one between Marcellinus (#29) and Marcellus I (#30) during the 4th century Diocletian persecution and interminably long conclaves, account for this ~57 year discrepancy. At first sight, 57 years over a two millennium period does not seem that much. But this actually turns out to be, on average, a 79 day *sede vacante* between each pope.

According to the current rules, the conclave to elect a new pope has to be convened within 15-20 days following the death of a pope. The *sede vacante* prior to Benedict XVI was 17 days. The four prior *sede vacantes* were, respectively, 18, 20, 18 and 19 days. So it is safe to say that long interregnums are definitely becoming a thing of the past.

The average length of reign for the 265 popes is 7.2 years – Pius IX's (#256) 31 year 7 month reign having been the longest and the original Stephen II's (#92) four days the shortest. The average regnal lengths for the ten most prevalent names are shown in graphical form on the next page – their names in descending order of prevalence starting at the left.

'Pius,' thanks to IX (#256 with 31.5 years), VI (#251 with 24.5 years), VII (#252 with 23.4 years) and XII (#261 with 19.6 years), stands head-and-shoulders above the rest with an average regnal length of 13.5 years. Even 'John Paul,' skewed as it is with but two instances, can not better this – their average being 13.2 years. Only the seven instances of 'Alexander,' where five of the pontificates exceeded ten years, comes even close with an average of 10.7 years.

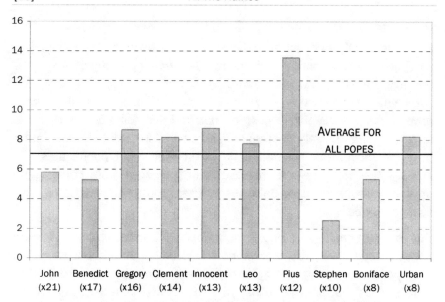

Average lengths of reign for the ten most prevalent names,
with 7.2 years being the average for all preceding popes.

The domination of the name 'Pius' since the late 1700s, as mentioned in Chapter III, cannot be underestimated. Pius VI (#251) and VII (#252) held office between them for a consecutive period of 47 years and 11 months. During the 103 year period between 15 February 1775 and 19 February 1878, there were four popes named 'Pius' who between them reigned for 81 years: i.e., 79% of the time.

John XXIII's (#262) quip about nearly all popes named 'John' having brief pontificates is indeed true in that they come in below the average. But 'Benedict,' 'Boniface' and 'Stephen' come in even lower. Benedict XVI (#266), elected three days after his 78th birthday, is the 5th oldest pope to have been elected during the last 500 years – Clement X (#240), elected in 1670, 75 days short of his 80th birthday being the oldest. Given his vast scholarship, he no doubt knew that 'Benedicts' have had even shorter pontificates than 'John.' Is it possible that future popes may think twice about assuming the name 'Pius,' following John's quip, given the implication that they hope to have a long pontificate?

WHY THE NUMBERING OF THE 'JOHNS' DO NOT ADD UP

John (Angelo) XXIII (#262) provided the cardinals who had elected him with a detailed explanation as to why he was resurrecting a long dormant and possibly tarnished name. Towards the end of this, he made the surprising statement that: *"Twenty-two Johns of indisputable legitimacy have [been Pope], and almost all had a brief pontificate."* The true surprise being the claim that there had been 22 legitimate 'Johns' rather than the moderately accurate quip about their short pontificates. His primary goal here appeared to have been to unequivocally portray (and dismiss) the opportunistic Baldassare Cossa (p. 61), the prior John (XXIII), as an antipope.

But to claim that there had hitherto been 22 *indisputably legitimate* popes named 'John' was, at best, quite a stretch – unless, of course, the new pope knew something that was not common knowledge! The problem was that per the official Vatican records there would only have been 20 legitimate 'Johns' – if Baldassare was now being categorically deemed an antipope.

Yes, there had been two other 'Johns,' one in 844 and the other in 997, but they had both already been castigated as antipopes during their lifetimes. Angelo, per his wont, may have been trying to be charitable towards the two antipopes. But this would have contradicted Vatican history and protocol.

There is a legend of sorts that there might have been an undocumented 'John,' with an ephemeral four month pontificate, in between John (Pietro) XIV (#137) and John XV (#138) – as discussed below. Angelo may have been counting this phantom Pope John. But that still leaves one unaccounted for. Possibly, though it is highly unlikely, he was alluding to the apocryphal, but always beguiling, Pope Joan – who per the legend held office in the 850s as a Pope John.

Maybe it was nothing other than a simple, spur of the moment, misstatement (well outside the sphere of infallibility) – given that he intended to be the 23rd. Per the prodigious dignity afforded to popes, there appears to have been no public questioning of his statement either by the cardinals present or the Vatican.

Suffice to say that Angelo's (possibly throwaway) statement further muddied what had, since the late 990s, been considerable confusion about the succession of the 'Johns.' The list below of all of the 'Johns' (with consecutive occurrences highlighted) helps underscore what the issues have been when it comes to the numbering of the legitimate popes named 'John' – following that of John (Pietro) XIV (#137).

	SEQ. #		REIGN	GAP: # POPES, YEARS
1.	#53	John I *the martyr* (p.9)	523-526	
2.	#56	John II (Mercurius)	533-535	2, 7 years
3.	#61	John III (Catelinus)	561-574	4, 26 years
4.	#72	John IV	640-642	10, 66 years
5.	#82	John V	685-686	9, 43 years
6.	#85	John VI	701-705	2, 15 years
7.	#86	John VII	705-707	*successive*
i.		Antipope John	844	
8.	#108	John VIII	872-882	21, 165 years
9.	#117	John IX	898-900	8, 16 years
10.	#123	John X	914-928	5, 14 years
11.	#126	John XI	931-935	2, 3 years
12.	#131	John XII (Octavian)	955-964	4, 20 years
13.	#134	John XIII	965-972	2, 1 year
14.	#137	John XIV (Pietro)	983-984	2, 11 years
x.		*the phantom John*	985	
15.	#138	John XV	985-996	*successive*, 1 y
ii.		Antipope John *(XVI)* - *Philagathos*	997-998	
16.	#141	John XVII (John Sicco)	1003-1003	2, 7 years
17.	#142	John XVIII (Giovani Fasanus)	1003-1009	*successive*
18.	#145	John XIX (Romanus)	1024-1032	2, 15 years
19.	#188	John XXI (Pedro)	1276-1277	42, 244 years
20.	#197	John XXII (Jacques)	1316-1334	8, 39 years
iii.		Antipope John *(XXIII)* - *Baldassare*	1410-1415	
21.	#262	John XXIII (Angelo)	1958-1963	64, 624 years

John (Pietro) XIV, appointed by the Holy Roman Emperor, was ousted eight months into his reign by antipope Boniface (VII) [p. 26]. Boniface died, abruptly, eleven months later. Soon afterwards, a Roman cardinal was installed as John XV (#138). But the 1917 *'Catholic Encyclopedia'* mentions 11th/12th century chroniclers and cataloguers who, however, *believed* that there was yet another pope named 'John' in between Boniface and John XV.

The encyclopedia, though, points out (correctly) that, while this mysterious pope John did not exist, it explains the subsequent problems related to enumerating the later 'Johns.' As if to confirm this, the encyclopedia assigns dual numbers for all the 'Johns' between John XV (XVI) and John XIX (XX) – a practice adopted by some earlier historians. This dual numbering convention is, however, not used by the more recent reference works.

It is now believed that the mysterious John came about due to a 11th/12th century misreading of the *Liber Pontificalis* narrative of John XIV's pontificate. It listed both the eight month duration of his papacy as well as the four months he spent in prison when ousted by Boniface (VII). The four months mentioned appear to have been interpreted as the papacy of another 'John' – given the rarity of seeing two time periods quoted for the same pope. This is indeed consistent with the time line evidence which shows that there would not have been time for another papacy, even one of four months, in between the death of Boniface and the election of John XV.

To exacerbate matters, three years after John XV's death, there was to be a short duration antipope named John (XVI) who tried to usurp Gregory V (#139). Gregory, once reinstated, made this John pay a heavy price for his indiscretion. The antipope, previously excommunicated by the Western bishops, was now severely assaulted, deprived of his sight, deposed and imprisoned. Consequently, there should not have been much doubt that this John was certainly considered to be an usurping antipope. But five years, later John Sicco elected to be John XVIII – defying the custom of reappropriating the ordinals of prior antipopes. Angelo, on the other hand, imposed this 'right' and reappropriated Baldassare's ordinals.

273 years later, the erudite Doctor Pedro exacerbated matters by opting to be John XXI – though there had never been a 'XX' pope or antipope. Given his background, he had either given this choice of numbering considerable thought or very little [p. 59]. It is said that he was reluctant to be pope – seeing it as interfering with his academic interests.

Consequently, he may not have been inclined to devote too much effort to determine what the right ordinal should have been.

He may have been aware of the phantom John and the dual numbering scheme that ensued with 'XV' also being known as 'XVI.' What he thus did was to accept the higher number even though it was out of synch from its inception and inaccurate because of the antipope 'XVI.' Pedro, as can be seen from the list above, was the 19th legitimate pope named 'John.' If the numbers were not so out of whack, Angelo should have been 'XXI' – thus obviating any mention of 22 'Johns' of indisputable legitimacy.

THE POPES NAMED 'SIXTUS'

Within the context of papal names, 'Sixtus/Xystus' has singular significance. This is so because:

1.   It was the first name to reoccur, not just once, but twice – and the only name to be repeated until 483.

2.   It is a name that has intimated that early Church historians may have indulged in some spin doctoring to enhance the propitiousness of some papal names.

3.   It is a name that suggests that priests in the early Roman church may have assumed a priestly name when ordained.

4.   It is a name that is now unlikely to be ever again assumed.

5.   It is a name that has been unfairly manipulated to associate the papacy with the dreaded '666.'

6.   It is a name that has global significance outside its traditional papal connotations in that the term 'Sistine,' as in the chapel and Raphael's Madonna [Fig. 21], pertain to 'Sixtus.'

Consequently, it would be remiss not to have a brief look at the five popes that have borne this name.

Sixtus I (#7) was elected, most likely by his fellow presbyters, at a time when the Roman church was still being governed collegiately by a group of senior presbyters. His father's name is said to have been 'Pastor.' He is traditionally credited, per *Liber Pontificalis* (despite chronological disconnects), with decreeing that only priests may touch the sacred vessels and with adding the *Sanctus* (holy) hymn to the "Eucharistic Prayer." It is also claimed that he prescribed that bishops summoned to

Figure 21: Pope St. Sixtus II (#24) in the c. 1513 *'Sistine Madonna'* by Raphael, where the 'Sistine' as with the chapel refers to Sixtus. It was painted above the altar for the Benedictine monastery church of San Sisto in Piacenza, N. Italy, which housed some of Sixtus II's relics -- where 'Sisto' also alludes to Sixtus. Commissioned by Julius II (#217) – nephew of Sixtus IV (#213) . Now in Dresden, Germany.

Rome must posses a 'papal' letter confirming their ongoing status when returning to their diocese to prove that they had not been deposed while in Rome.

Tradition maintains that he was martyred (though this was unlikely) and buried under St. Peter's Basilica. It is also said that in 1132 Innocent II (#165), at the bidding of the residents of Alife [Italy], granted them Sixtus I's relics. But the mule carrying the relics from Rome refused to go beyond Alatri [Italy]. So, the relics were interned at the Alatri Cathedral with Alfie just getting a finger bone. Some others say that some of his relics were also taken to France. His feast day is April 6 – '6' being the hallmark of this name. (Some others maintain that his feast day is 3 days earlier.)

Sixtus II – a true martyr
Sixtus II (#24) is thought to have been Greek – possibly because of his original name 'Xystus' [p. 35], or due to a confusion with an author of that name who had been a follower of the Greek mathematician and philosopher Pythagoras. He was elected by the Roman clergy possibly in concert with some of the Christian laity 28 days after the death of Stephen I (#23). In time, an interregnum of such duration would come to be seen as rather quick.

He, like his predecessor, did not see a need to rebaptize those originally baptized by priests hence deemed to be heretical. However, unlike

Stephen, he, more affable, was willing to compromise to preclude a schism with the churches in North Africa and Asia Minor. Per Sixtus II, the acceptance of lapsed Christians without rebaptism would be the norm. Churches that wished so were, however, permitted to insist on rebaptism.

Emperor Valerian (253-260) who had started off by being sympathetic to Christians reinstated persecution in mid-257. Christians were banned from congregating in cemeteries and were expected to participate in Roman religious functions. In 258, he became more ruthless and ordered the execution of all Christian clergy and deacons.

On August 6, while conducting a service at a cemetery, Sixtus, who was seated in his bishop's chair [*i.e., cathedra*], was suddenly attacked by imperial guards and beheaded along with four deacons. He is thus a revered martyr. He was originally buried in the papal crypt in the catacombs of St. Callistus (#16). During the 6th century, his relics were moved to Rome's San Sisto Vecchio.

Documents initially attributed to him, other than a letter to Dionysius, Bishop of Alexandria, were in reality written by others. His feast day is August 6 – the day of his martyrdom (which coincidently is yet another instance of a '6' figuring in the story of a 'Sixtus.') Some have the feast day falling one day later on August 7.

Sixtus III – believed to have founded Rome's first monastery

His father's name is also said to have been 'Xystus' thus indicating that he may have also been a priest at some point. Though no records exist, Sixtus III (#44) was most likely a rising cleric during the time of Zosimus (#41). He, like Zosimus, is said to have originally believed in the Pelagianist 'redemption-through-free will' heresy. In 418, the African bishops and the Western Emperor forced Zosimus to recant his approval of Pelagianism.

Zosimus did so via a document called the '*Tractoria.*' Sixtus is said to have written to St. Augustine of Hippo [Algeria] (354-430), the chief opponent of Pelagianism, that he too had become a convert after reading the '*Tractoria.*' It is this supposed correspondence that intimates that Sixtus was already a cleric of note c. 418.

The First Council of Ephesus [Turkey] was convened in 431 by Eastern Emperor Theodosius II (408 - 450) to resolve the increasingly fiery Nestorianism controversy after Celestine I's (#43) denouncement of it in 430. Nestorianism maintained that Christ existed as two separate beings, one human, the other divine, sharing the same body. Nestorians insisted on referring to the Virgin Mary as the 'mother of Christ' (Greek *Christotokos*) as opposed to the accepted 'mother of God' *(Theotokos)*.

The Council, presided over by Cyril (Patriarch) of Alexandria, condemned Nestorianism as false. It affirmed Christ being one person, both God and man, and hence, the validity of the *Theotokos* designation. The Council also rejected Pelagianism. It was a fractious council with many accusations and countercharges which led to the first schism within the Church – with what would be the Assyrian Church of the East parting ways with the rest.

Letters written by Sixtus shortly after he became pope made references to communiqués by Celestine dealing with the aftermath of the Council. This indicates that Sixtus was close to his predecessor and may have even helped Celestine deal with the fallout from Ephesus. [Neither Celestine nor Sixtus attended the Council.]

The patriarchs of Alexandria [Egypt] and Antioch [Turkey] had been at odds before, during and after Ephesus. With the Assyrian Church already in schism, Sixtus was anxious to avoid further disruptions. With Theodosius II's help, Sixtus orchestrated a tenuous peace between the two patriarchs – culminating in the 'Symbol of Union' accord of 433. He credited St. Peter for this success.

Shortly afterwards, Sixtus thwarted attempts by the new Archbishop of Constantinople [Turkey] to assert dominion over the 'Balkans.' To preclude future overtures, he informed the Archbishop that he was not to entertain any bishops from that region unless they had credentials from the pope's 'Balkans' vicar – the Bishop of Thessalonica [NE Greece].

With help from the Imperial court, Sixtus mobilized an ambitious program to revitalize Rome – still scarred from the Visigoth sacking of 410. He expanded Liberius' (#36) Basilica Liberian to be Santa Maria Maggorie – to honor the Virgin Mary after the Ephesus confirmation of her stature as 'mother-of-God.' He also added the octagonal baptistery to the San Giovanni in Laterano to glorify the recent victories over heresies. He is believed to have founded the first Roman monastery.

He is buried in Rome's San Lorenzo fuori le Mura. His feast day is March 28. Since Sixtus III can be interpreted as '6th III,' this peace-loving and committed pope is unjustly associated by some with the maligned '666.'

Sixtus IV – redeemed by the Sistine

If not for the Sistine and to a lesser extent Rome's Ponte Sisto bridge, this pope would be best remembered for authorizing the Spanish Inquisition (1478), appointing the merciless Tomás *(the-hammer-of-heretics)* de Torquemada as its grand inquisitor (1483) and egregious nepotism. Mandell Creighton (1843-1901), a onetime Bishop of London and a papal historian of note, commented that Sixtus IV (#213) [Fig. 7] *"lowered the moral tone of Europe."* He set the tone for a series of rather worldly Renaissance popes.

Francesco della Rovere was from a humble family of fishermen plying their trade around the coasts of Genoa [Italy]. He joined the Franciscans at an early age and went on to become an acclaimed intellectual, lecturer and preacher. In 1464, he was elected Minister General of the Franciscans. He became a cardinal in 1467. His election to pope is said to have been facilitated by the effusive gifts and promises of his 'nephews' during the conclave. He opted to be 'Sixtus' since the conclave that elected him had convened on the feast day of St. Sixtus II.

In common with his two predecessors, he tried to mount a crusade against the Ottoman Turks. Though he expended considerable resources to raise a naval fleet, the support he received from other European powers was scant – as was the efficacy of the fleet. In addition, he continued an ongoing wrangle with the King of France as to the true extent of papal jurisdiction within France – victory again eluding him.

He was, however, to be inordinately successful in enriching his family – in particular a large band of 'nephews,' at least two of them said to be his sons. Sixtus appointed 34 cardinals – six of them 'nephews' – Giuliano della Rovere, the future Julius II (#217), being one. An attempt to allot a part of the Papal States to another 'nephew' led to a confrontation with the abutters to the North – the Republic of Florence.

This escalated into the 1478 *"Pazzi Conspiracy,"* which led to the attack on the Medici brothers during the Easter Sunday Mass at the Dumo. Lorenzo *il Magnifico* [father of Leo X (#218)] was badly injured. His brother Giuliano [father of Clement VII (#220)] died from nineteen stab wounds. The pope, implicated in the conspiracy, reacted by declaring war against Florence – in time Venice and Ferrara [Italy] getting dragged into the fray.

It is said that Sixtus encouraged and taxed prostitution to finance his building projects, military forays and family 'trust' fund. To his credit though, he vastly modernized Rome (with the Sistine but just one example), revitalized the Papal States, formed the Sistine choir, created the Vatican archives, authorized the feast of the Immaculate Conception and furthered the lot of mendicant orders [e.g., Franciscans, Carmelites, Dominicans]. He fell ill in mid-June 1484 and died on August 12 still railing against all the Italians he was still at odds with. He was buried at the Vatican.

Sixtus V – the iron pope

Sixtus V (#228), like his prior namesake, was a high-ranking Franciscan. He assumed that name because of this connection. There are also other parallels between these two. They are both from modest backgrounds. They both gained early notoriety for their scholarship and oratory. IV authorized the Spanish Inquisition while V was sent to Venice [Italy] in 1557 as its inquisitor general by Paul IV (#224). A century apart, they both did much to enhance Rome's appearance and amenities – with V noted for his infrastructure improvements such as roads and aqueducts [e.g., *Acqua Felice* – 'Felice' being his birth name].

Despite their immense civic initiatives, both were to be intensely unpopular albeit for different reasons. IV's downfall was nepotism. V's nepotism was limited to his sister. Despite her original modest roots, she was to become one of the wealthiest of Roman females during her brother's pontificate.

V's primary weakness was his unremitting ruthlessness – a trait that he had exhibited in Venice in his role as inquisitor general. Though this helped him stamp out rampant lawlessness in the Papal States, it was at the cost of earning a reputation summed up by the 19th century Italian poet Giuseppe Gioacchino Belli as: *"Among all those who held the charge of God's vicar, a quarrelsome, tough, crazy pope such as Pope Sixtus had never been seen before."*

Felice Peretti was born in a village on Italy's Adriatic coast, on December 13, 1521, to a farming family with Balkan roots. He had an uncle who was a Franciscan. He himself joined that order at the age of twelve in the town of Montalto – thus earning his sobriquet *'Felice di Montalto.'* By 1550, his brilliance and asceticism was being noted by Church leaders. Paul IV appointed him inquisitor general for Venice. But his fervency was such that the Venetians successfully clamored to get rid of him. He was reinstated in 1560 by Pius IV (#225). Sent to Spain as an inquisitor, he crossed swords with the head of that delegation, Ugo Boncompagni – the future Gregory XIII (#227).

The next pope, Pius V (#226), a grand inquisitor himself, proved to be a mentor and eventually made him a cardinal in 1570. During Gregory XIII's reign, 'Cardinal Montalto' went into self-imposed exile in his Roman villa and occupied himself writing a book on the scholarly 4th century Bishop of Milan, St. Ambrose [c. 338-397]. A group of supporters who knew him prior to his exile engineered his election.

As pope he was driven, zealous and unyielding. He restored law and order to the Papal States – albeit at the costs of innumerable lives. He regulated food prices, minimized Vatican spending, facilitated trade and initiated far reaching urban revitalization projects. But he also raised taxes, indulged simony and flirted with usury. Despite the cost of his building projects, he still managed to amass a huge fortune. Though it was a relatively short pontificate, he succeeded in streamlining the Vatican bureaucracy, making bishops more accountable and enlarging the College of Cardinals to 70.

He died from complications from malaria at the newly built Quirinal Palace [Rome] – the first pope to die there. He was buried in Rome's Santa Maria Maggiore – a church founded by Sixtus III. Though effective as a pope, Sixtus V was intensely disliked. This is reflected in Belli's poem, earlier quoted, which ends with the barb: *"Because not too soon another pope may have the whim of naming himself Sixtus the Sixth."*

POSSIBLE NAMES OF FUTURE POPES

The five cardinals deemed to be most *papabile* by Paddy Power [p. 5], as of Spring 2008, in descending order of probability, were: Angelo Scola [Venice, Italy], Christoph Schönborn [Vienna, Austria], Oscar Andrés Rodríguez Maradiaga [Honduras], Jorge Mario Bergoglio [Argentina] and Francis Arinze [Nigeria]. Paddy Power was indeed 'in the money' with both the name 'Benedict' and Cardinal Ratzinger as a *papabile* in 2005. Consequently, these rankings do have some credibility and standing particularly given that there is real money at stake here.

If elected, none of them could do a 'Marcellus' (#223) and retain their birth name since none of their names or variants are part of the current papal roll – with names referencing Christ [as in 'Christoph'] being notably absent. The there is always the possibility that the new pope may buck the trend and either retain his existing name or slightly more likely come up with a new name altogether -- possibly two-fold such as 'Pius John.' To have a Pope Angelo or Christoph would be refreshing and could imbue a whole new, and some would even contend much needed, 21st century aura to the papacy.

Each of these *papabile*, however, have some interesting options as to existing papal names they could assume given their names and backgrounds. Take Angelo Scola. The previous 'Angelo' was the much loved and now beatified John XXIII – who, like Scola, was the Patriarch of Venice. So John XXIV could be a possibility – but Scola, a conservative, may feel that the last 'John' was a tad too liberal.

Scola was made a cardinal by John Paul II (#265). He has been closely associated with the *'Pontifical John Paul II Institute for Studies on Marriage and the Family'* – a private, post-graduate, theological college. John Paul II's conservative credentials are sound, while John Paul I was also a Patriarch of Venice. So, John Paul III is another possibility.

Christoph Schönborn, an exacting theologian as befits a Dominican, was a protégé of Joseph Ratzinger [i.e., Benedict XVI (#260)]. St. Pius V (#226), considered a great but harsh pope, was also a Dominican. So was Innocent V (#186). Pius V was the last but one pope to be canonized -- Pius X (#258) being the last. Therefore, 'Pius,' 'Benedict' or 'Innocent' would be logical choices for Christoph – if elected.

Oscar Maradiaga, when 19, joined the Catholic religious order *Salesians of Don Bosco* ('Salesians'). He is somewhat of a liberal. The Salesians was founded in the late 19th century by St. *John Bosco (1815-1888)*. Hence, John XXIV could be appropriate. He may, on the other hand, wish to highlight his Spanish heritage. The last two Spanish popes were the Borgias – Alexander VI (#215) being the notoriously depraved Rodrigo de Borja. But then there is the Portuguese Pedro *'Hispano'* [i.e., *Spanish]* Julião – John XXI (#188) [p. 59] -- another nod for John XXIV.

There have been two 'Alexanders' since Rodrigo. Fabio Chigi, who was born in Siena [Italy], chose to be Alexander VII (#238) since Alexander III (#171) was also a Sienese. Three popes later, Pietro Vito Ottoboni opted to be Alexander VIII (#242) to pay homage to 'III,' who had been a mentor. The name 'Callistus,' however, has not been assumed since Alfonso de Borja – whose only major *faux pas* was to make two nephews, one of them Rodrigo, cardinals. But 'Callistus,' best known for the Roman catacombs, would now be considered too dated by most.

Jorge Bergoglio is described as being a conservative in the mold of John Paul II and Benedict XVI – John Paul II having made him a cardinal. So, John Paul III and Benedict XVII are possibilities. He is also an ex-chemist from a country with Spanish legacy. But it is doubtful whether he would consider 'John' in honor of Pedro *'Hispano.'*

If elected, Francis Arinze will probably be the first black pope, but not the first with an African pedigree. St. Victor I (#14) is believed to have been born in North Africa in a region that today would be Tunisia. Some, influenced by the *Liber Pontificalis* statement that he was African, claim that St. Miltiades (#32) was black and born in Africa. Others, more critical, believe that he was Roman with some African roots. St. Gelasius I (#49), who was not black, was born in Rome of African parents.

Though Victor I was a historic pope, the first to contemplate papal primacy, it is unlikely that 'Victor' would now be deemed an appropriate name for a 21st century pope – particularly with the name 'Victor Emmanuel' synonymous with Italian unification of the 1860s which resulted in the loss of the Papal States. 'Miltiades' and 'Gelasius,' like 'Callistus,' sound too dated. Consequently, it is difficult to see Francis Arinze opting for any of these three 'African' names.

John Paul visited Nigeria twice and was the pope that made Arinze a cardinal. So, John Paul III would make sense. But he has an ecumenical bent and his titular church as cardinal is Rome's San Giovanni della Pigna. Hence, 'John' is another possibility.

In general, 'John,' 'John Paul,' 'Benedict,' 'Pius,' 'Clement,' 'Paul,' 'Leo,' 'Gregory' and 'Innocent' fall into the 'good name' category – as would two-fold permutations of these names. The only real issue with 'Nicholas' would appear to be the association with Santa Claus. 'Peter' continues to be off-limits, independent of Malachy prophecy [p. 5]. 'Formosus,' 'Sixtus,' 'Marcus,' 'Urban' and 'Julius' are likely to be considered incongruous for a modern pope. Many of the other names, for example 'Pelagius,' 'Vigilius,' Eutychian and Zacharias, would come across as anachronistic. But it would also be invigorating to have a new name or two – an 'Angelo,' a 'Christoph' or a 'Matthew.'

V:
RATIONALES FOR CHOOSING THE ASSUMED NAMES

artolomeo Alberto (Mauro) Cappellari, a monk in the Benedictine Camaldolese order, was unexpectedly elected pope on February 2, 1831, following a fractious 50-day conclave. In 1805 Mauro had been appointed abbot of Rome's San Gregorio (St. Gregory) Magno al Celio monastery. St. Gregory I 'the Great' (#64) had been a monk there, the monastery having been built on what were the grounds of his ancestral home.

Around 1814, Mauro had become the head of the 'Congregation for the Propagation of Faith,' which had been founded in 1622 by Gregory XV (#235). Mauro chose to be Gregory XVI (#255) in honor of these two popes who were associated with significant facets of his earlier life. He is, to date, the last monk to be elected pope. He is also the last who was not a bishop when elected.

The scholarly Enea Silvio Piccolomini, 'Cardinal of Siena,' when elected by acclamation in August 1458, chose to be Pius II (#211), because the protagonist in Virgil's (29-19 BC) epic poem *Aeneid* describes himself as *pius Aeneas* – 'Aeneas' being the Latin form of his first name [p. 74].

Francesco Todeschini Piccolomini, in 1503, opted to be Pius III (#216), because Pius II was his maternal uncle.

Barnaba Niccolò Maria Luigi ('Gregorio') Chiaramonti, born a count, was elected pope, albeit as a compromise candidate, on March 14, 1800, after a 14 week conclave in Venice [Italy]. The prior pope, Pius VI (#251), a

Figure 22: Gregory I 'the Great' (#64), depicted here, in a customary scholarly pose, c. 1610, by Carlo Saraceni (c. 1570-1620) and others. [Now at the Galleria Nazionale d'Arte Antica in Rome.] The dove symbolizes the Holy Spirit whispering God's words for transcription by Gregory. He is believed to be the first monk to become a pope. Gregory XVI (#255), twelve centuries later, was the last.

family friend, was responsible for his bishopric and cardinalate. In recognition, Gregorio chose to be Pius VII (#252). In 1816, he made Francesco Saverio Castiglioni a cardinal. Thirteen years later, Francesco became the new pope. Intending to continue the traditions of Pius VII, he opted to be Pius VIII (#254). He was the third 'Pius' in 54 years – his two successors having reigned for a total of 47 years and 11 months.

Fabio Chigi, in 1655, chose to be Alexander VII (#238) because he and Alexander III (#171) were both from Siena [Italy] – paying no regard to the very negative notoriety of Alexander (Borja) VI (#215). Thirty four years later,

Figure 23: Pius VII (#252) was the son of a Count from Northern Italy. He joined the Benedictines and assumed the name 'Gregorio' (Gregory). Pius VI (#251), a family friend, made him a cardinal at 43. His papacy was plagued by pressure from France's Napoleon I Bonaparte (1769-1821). His 23 year pontificate is the 6th longest to date.

Pietro Vito Ottoboni opted to be Alexander VIII (#242), because he considered himself a protégé of Alexander VII.

Angelo Giuseppe Roncalli, then 77, did not enter the October 25, 1958 conclave expecting to be elected pope [p.62]. Cardinal Giuseppe Siri, from Genoa [Italy], 25 years younger than Angelo, with considerable support from the Vatican curia ['bureaucracy'], was the presumptive. But his age proved to be an impediment. If elected, Siri might have been pope for 30 years.

Angelo gained favor as a short-term, transitional prospect. On the last ballot of the second day, Angelo was ahead -- but three shy of the 'two-thirds plus one' votes he needed to win. With 51 cardinals in attendance, Angelo needed 35 votes to be elected. That night his supporters assured him that the necessary votes would be forthcoming the next day. He thus had time that night to think about what name he wished to be known by. He even prepared some notes to justify his selection of John XXIII (#262) – albeit with an inaccurate count of the legitimately elected 'Johns' prior to him [p. 82].

Angelo stated six reasons for his choice of name – the first and foremost being that it was the name of his father, Giovanni Battista (John the Baptist) Roncalli. He said that it was the name of the humble parish church where their family received their baptisms. Two of his biographers, however, state that Roncalli was baptized in the church of Santa Maria (Saint Mary) of Brusico in his birth town of Sotto il Monte [Italy]. There was indeed an older San Giovanni Batista parish church on a nearby hillside. That was probably where his father was baptized. Hence his name.

Angelo pointed out that it was, also the solemn name of numerous cathedrals around the world – key among these being the Bishop of Rome's own official cathedral the Basilica di San Giovanni in Laterano (St. John Lateran). He pointed out that it was the most used of the papal names and that there had been 22 unquestionably legitimate popes of this name – most of them having had short pontificates. There had, however, only been twenty legitimate popes called 'John.' Furthermore, on average, popes with the names 'Benedict,' 'Boniface' and 'Stephen' have had shorter pontificates than those named 'John' [p. 81].

Joseph Alois Ratzinger, when elected on April 19, 2005, took the name Benedict XVI (#266). He wished to pay homage to Benedict XV's (#259) commitment to peace during World War I and to also show his

Figure 24: The façade of the Basilica di San Giovanni in Laterano (Basilica of St John Lateran), the official cathedral of the Bishop of Rome, the pope – the oldest and highest ranked of Rome's four major basilicas which includes St. Peter's.

admiration for St. Benedict of Nursia (c. 489-c. 547), the pioneer of Christian monasticism. Taking the lead from Roncalli, he is said to have also added that Benedict XV had served only briefly – i.e., seven years and four months. This was germane given that Ratzinger had turned 78 three days earlier. He thus became the 5th oldest pope to have been elected during the last 500 years.

MULTIPLE RATIONALES FOR CHOOSING AN ASSUMED NAME

There are 125 documented instances of popes assuming a new name upon being elected. With 67 of these popes, the rationale for their choice of name is known with a high degree of certainty – either through their own disclosure [e.g., John XXIII (#262)], credible contemporaneous reports or via relatively straightforward deduction [e.g., John II (#56) taking the name of the recently martyred pope]. With the other 58, it is a matter of supposition – albeit using the 67 known scenarios for guidance.

The various reasons, whether known or supposed, for assuming a particular name can be grouped into nine main categories. These were:

1. To honor a *mentor*: In particular, a prior pope responsible for appointing the pope-elect a cardinal, archbishop or bishop. In some instances, the mentoring may have been at an earlier juncture, such as a then bishop promoting the career of a young priest. In the case of Paul V (#234), Paul III (#221) had been not his, but his father's mentor. Benedict XI's (#195) mentor was Boniface VIII (#194) – whose birth name was *Benedetto* Caetani. There are 21 instances, 20 known and one supposed, of mentor-influenced assumed names. The remaining nineteen instances are discussed below.

2. To propagate the name of a *family member*: There are ten instances of these with three being suppositions. Of the seven known, four pertain to prior popes [e.g., Benedict VIII (#144) was Benedict IX's (#146) 'uncle' or possibly even father], while in the case of John XXIII (#262), it was his father, a lifelong farmer. See Page 100.

3. To commemorate a canonized pope whose *feast day* coincided with the conclave that elected the new pope: There are four known instances when this rationale was used. These were: Stephen IX (#155), elected on August 2 the feast day of St. Stephen I (#23); Martin V (#207), elected on (or very close to) the original feast day [i.e., Nov. 12] of St. Martin I (#74); Clement XI (#244), elected on November 23 the Western feast day of St Clement I (#4) and Sixtus IV (#213), where the conclave that elected him convened on August 6, the feast day of Sixtus II (#24).

4. To pay homage to and possibly also to indicate a desire to emulate a prominent pope from the past: e.g., Gregory V (#139), the first German-born pope, who cited his admiration for Gregory I 'the Great' (#64). There are twenty instances (sixteen known) when the desire to pay homage was the motive for choosing a particular assumed name. See page 101 for more details.

5. To acclaim a prior pope from the same *country, region or city*: For example, Clement VIII (#232), with his deep Florentine roots acclaiming the previous pope from Florence, Clement (Medici) VII (#220); Alexander VII (#238) and III (#171) were both from Sienna [Italy], while Urban IV (#183) and II (#160) were French. Gregory XIII

(#227) and XV (#235) were both from Bologna [Italy] – with XIII also having been an early mentor. There are 15 such geographic associations – albeit with ten based on supposition. For example, did Hadrian V (#187), a former papal legate to England, chose that name because Hadrian I (#96) and (Nicholas Breakspear) IV (#170) both had ties to England? See page 103 for the remaining instances in this category.

6. To make a subtle *political* statement: There are nine possible instances of such names – albeit all but one based on supposition since the object in each case appears to have been to convey a veiled statement that would only be appreciated by the cognoscenti. For example, did Giovanni Coniulo choose to be Gelasius II (#162) to remind emperors of the 'two powers' theory that had been put forward by Gelasius I (#49) six centuries earlier? More on this and the other eight instances can be found on page 104.

7. To empathize with *early Church leaders* and possibly to derive inspiration or fortitude from their deeds: For example, the name 'Silvester' has only occurred thrice. Silvester I (#33), 150 years after his death, started to gain a *legendary* reputation of having been Emperor Constantine I's (306-337) advisor, confidante and savior. It is likely that Silvester II (#140) and III (#147) assumed that name to show their empathy with the pope, who had such a close relationship with the most pivotal of the Roman Emperors. In addition to the two 'Silvesters,' there are ten other such possibilities that are listed on page 103.

8. To reflect a facet from pope-elect's *background* that coincided with that of an earlier pope: Such as the Gregory XVI (#255) example cited at the start of this chapter. Other examples being: Nicholas III (#189) was a Cardinal-Deacon at Rome's San *Nicola* in Carcere (prison) church while Nicholas V (#209) was a protégé of Bishop *Niccolò* Albergati of Bologna. Sixtus V (#228) and Sixtus IV (#213) were both Franciscans, whereas Benedict XIII (#246) and Benedict XI (#195) were Dominicans. There are sixteen other instances [p. 107] that fall into this category with fifteen of these being logical, but unverifiable, inferences.

9. To express rapport with a prior pope: For example, Julius III (#222) who is said to have believed that he had the same temperament as

the fiery but highly cultured 'warrior pope' Julius II (#217). Clement IX (#239) chose his name to denote he approved of and was a believer in the reconciliation policies pursued by Clement VIII (#232). Both these Clements were also from Tuscany [Italy] – which may have been an additional impetus. There are nine other possible instances that fall into this category – which are discussed on page 106.

There are two popes whose rationales for choosing the name 'Pius' does not fall into any of the above categories. Pius II (#211) was inspired by a literary reference [p. 94], while Pius IV (#225) wanted to be known for his piety. With the exception of these two popes, plus Pius III (#216), who was the nephew of Pius II, the other eight instances of 'Pius' being assumed were based on either mentoring or homage – with an even 4-4 split. 'Clement' also was chosen four times (with three in a row) for mentoring, but never for homage *per se*.

'Eugene' was assumed but twice, and in both cases it is believed that it was to reflect an aspect of the pope-elect's 'prior life.' Eugene IV (#208) and Eugene III (#168) had both been monks, while III may have assumed that name because Eugene I (#75) was a long-term cleric. Similarly, both instances of 'Boniface' being assumed appear to be due to a Neapolitan thread between Boniface V (#69), VIII (#194) and IX (204).

Mentors and family members

In addition to Benedict XI (#195) and Paul V (#234) mentioned above, there are nineteen other pope-elects who assumed the name of a mentor – albeit with one of these, i.e., Celestine IV (#180), being a supposition.

Nothing is known of Celestine IV's early life. The belief that he was a nephew of Urban III (#173) cannot be collaborated, and he obviously did not want to be Urban IV. It is, however, known that he did become the chancellor of a church in Milan around 1220. Celestine III (#176) was pope from April 1191 to January 1198. It is thus very conceivable that Celestine III may have helped IV during the early stages of his ecclesiastical career. But there are no records of this.

With the exception of Pius IX (#256) (a.k.a. 'Pio Nono') and John Paul I (#264) (a.k.a. 'Gianpaolo'), the mentor in all the other seventeen instances was the prior pope of the same name. Pius VII (#252), during his 23 year pontificate, was a mentor to both Pius VIII (#254) and Pius IX (#256). They were separated by Gregory XVI's (#255) 15 year papacy. Pius VII made VIII a cardinal in 1816. Pius IX, born in 1792, was considerably younger and was only ordained a priest in 1819 – 19 years into Pius VII's papacy. So, rather than making him a bishop or a cardinal, Pius VII encouraged him during his early days as a priest. John Paul I honored John XXIII (#262) for making him a bishop and Paul VI (#263) for his elevation to Cardinal.

The other eighteen popes who assumed the name of their mentor, in alphabetical order, are: Alexander VIII (#242), Benedict XIV (#248), Celestine III (#176), Clement X (#240), Clement XII (#247), Clement XIII (#249), Clement XIV (#250), Gregory XIV (#230), Innocent XI (#241), Innocent XII (#243), Nicholas IV (#192), Paul IX (#224), Pius VII (#252), Pius VIII (#254), Pius IX (#256), Urban VI (#203) and Pius XII (#261).

In addition to acknowledging Pius XI's role as mentor, Pius XII also wanted to honor XI's unwavering commitment to furthering peace initiatives during what was the build up to WW II. Pius VIII, too, had an additional motive. He wanted to rekindle the traditions upheld by Pius VII.

When it comes to family connections, Innocent XIII (#245) was related to the Counts of Segni [Italy] dynasty that had produced *Innocent III* (#177), Gregory IX (#179) and Alexander IV (#182). 'Innocent' was most likely chosen because it was the oldest and the most illustrious. Honorius III (#178) was the great-uncle of Honorius IV (#191), Leo X (#218) was the maternal grand-uncle of Leo XI (#233), while Pius II (#211) was the maternal uncle of Pius III (#216). John XI (#126) was John XII's (#131) step-uncle. There are three possible familial connections that are undocumented but appear to have merit. These are: Anastasius III (#121) and IV (#169), Honorius I (#70) and II (#164), and Innocent II (#165) and III (#177).

Rendering reverence

The conclave to elect John Paul I's (#264) successor lasted two and a half days [Oct. 14 -16, 1978]. Judging by the number of times smoke was seen emanating from the Sistine Chapel chimney there were at least eight rounds of balloting. By the half-way point of this relatively short conclave, (the 2nd in two months) Karol Józef Wojtyla, Archbishop of Kraków [Poland] knew that his star was in the ascend. Thus, as with John XXIII (#262), he had time to mull over the name by which he wished to be known.

It is said that he confided in his longtime friend and now his electoral sponsor, Cardinal Franz Koenig of Vienna [Austria], that he might consider assuming the name 'Stanislaus' -- in honor of the sainted Polish martyr. Koening is said to have steered him away from that name -- most likely since it would have drawn unnecessary attention to the pope's nationality. He then elected to be John Paul II (#264) in honor of his short-lived and extremely popular predecessor, but also mentioned that he had gained strength and inspiration from Paul VI (#263). He, however, did not mention the 'liberal' John XXIII, the first named in the 'John Paul' combo, who had tried to reach out to the Soviets!

Benedict XVI's (#266) admiration for Benedict XV (#259) was discussed earlier, as was Gregory V's (#139) motives - where the desire to downplay his German nationality may have been the impetus for opting for an assumed name in the first place. Gregory VII (#158) and XIII (#227) were also showing their reverence to Gregory I 'the Great' (#64), whereas Leo XII (#253) gravitated towards the first of the three greats, Leo I (#45). Nicholas II (#156) opted for the remaining great, Nicholas I (#106).

Gregory VI (#149) bought his papacy from his unscrupulous godson Benedict IX (#146, #148 & #151) [p. 58]. It appears, however, that there was a sham election of sorts to ratify the transference of the papacy. It is said that the name 'Gregory,' in honor of the 'great,' was given to the new pope by those present at this gathering - as opposed to being chosen by the new pope. This was unusual to say the least, but there was nothing normal about this transference of office or the actions of the two popes involved.

'Mercurius,' when seeking a Christian replacement for his pagan name, chose to honor the recently martyred John I (#53) and became John II (#56). 'Catelinus' is believed to have done the same to become John III (#61). The next to assume the name, i.e., John XII (#131) did so because his step-uncle had been John XI (#126). Pietro Canepanova was the next to assume that name. He was chosen by the Holy Roman Emperor [p. 26]. Consequently, he may not have been related to any of the recent 'Johns.' Thus, his inspiration for becoming John XIV (#137) may again have been John I. If not, he may have been paying homage to John the Baptist or the Apostle. There is also a possibility that it may have been political [p.8].

It is believed that Innocent II (#165) was paying homage to Innocent I (#40), while Innocent IV (#181) intended to show his admiration for Innocent III's (#177) staunch stance on papal primacy - a right that he held dear.

Pietro Barbo, portrayed as vain, is said to have toyed with becoming Formosus II [p. 10]. But decorum prevailed and he elected to be Paul II (#212). Paul I (#94), an able administrator, was not a martyr or a particularly outstanding pope. Consequently, it has to be assumed that Pietro took the name of Rome's other Apostle, St. Paul, as opposed to that of the 94th pope. Gregory VI, Innocent II, John XII, John IV and Paul II are the five instances in this category that are based on supposition.

With Paul VI (#263), however, there is no doubt that he was reaching out to the Apostle. He was committed to the ecumenism that was being promoted by the Vatican II Council (1962-1965), over which he eventually presided. With his name, the new pope wished to remind people of St. Paul's efforts to reach out to the gentiles.

Leo XIII's (#257) motivation was to show his esteem for Leo XII (#253) – who had been pope when he had arrived in Rome, as a student, in 1824. Pius XI's (#260) rationale was similar. Pius IX (#256) had been pope when he was born, while he was ordained a priest during the papacy of Pius X (#258). He also liked the 'peaceful' connotation of that name. However, the pope whose policies he intended to pursue were those of his predecessor, Benedict XV (259).

The struggle to unify Italy, assimilating the papal states in the process, occurred during Pius IX's unprecedented 31 year reign. It was a harsh time for the pope, especially when he had to escape from Rome in disguise. Pius X's (#258) choice of name was to pay tribute to the degradations stoically endured by Pius IX.

Antonio (Michele) Ghislieri owed his election to Cardinal Carlo Borromeo, Pius IV's (#225) nephew. Ghislieri, to show his gratitude, assumed the name Pius V (#226) to honor Borromeo's uncle. Pius V, who died in May 1572, was canonized by Clement XI (#244) on May 24, 1712 – the first pope to be so honored in 400 years. Giovanni Angelo Braschi, when elected pope in 1775, assumed the name of the latest canonized pope – thus becoming Pius VI (#251).

Geographic intersections
In 1281, following a six month conclave that involved the kidnapping of cardinals to sway the vote, Simon de Brion, a French cardinal, was finally elected pope by the narrowest of margins. He had been born in the province of Touraine – whose capital was Tours. He chose to be 'Martin'

in honor of St. Martin of Tours, a 4th century Bishop of Tours, who during the 6th century became the patron saint of France (and soldiers).

Around the 13th century, papal scribes had confused the names of 'Marinus' with 'Martin' and had designated Marinus I (#109) and II (#129) as Martin II and III. Consequently, de Brion became Martin IV (#190) though he was but the second of that name.

This leaves nine other instances where a papal name is thought to be the result of a geographic intersection with a prior pope. For example, Boniface V (#69), VIII (#194) and IX (#204) have a Neapolitan connection. It appears to be the only discernable rationale as to why VIII and IX chose to be 'Boniface.' But this cannot be confirmed – hence the need to treat all nine of these instances as suppositions.

The Spanish Alfonso de Borja (Borgia) may have opted to be Callistus III (#210) because Callistus II (#163) had Spanish relatives. There might have even been an undocumented family connection. The French Jacques Duèze (or d'Euse) was appointed Cardinal Bishop of Porto [Portugal] in 1313. The following year Clement V (#196), the first Avignon [France] pope, died. There was to be a contentious two year interregnum before Jacques was finally elected to be the second in the Avignon line. He chose to be John XXII (#197) – most likely because John XXI (#188), the accidentally killed Pedro 'Hispano,' was the pope from Portugal [p. 59].

Clement V (#196) and IV (#184) were both French. Innocent V (#186) and IV (#181) had both spent time in Lyon [France] – IV while seeking refuge from Imperial interference in Rome. The next Innocent, i.e., VI (#200), a French Avignon pope, may have opted to continue this French theme.

This now leaves John (Pedro 'Hispano') XXII – who reactivated this name after a 244 year hiatus. The prior 'John,' i.e., 'Romanus' XIX (#145), was a Tusculan pope [p. 58]. Pedro was the Cardinal Bishop of Tusculum before becoming pope. Did he opt to be 'John' because of this Tusculum connection?

Veiled political statements

Giovanni Coniulo was elected at a time when the papacy was again being subject to Imperial harassment. The key issue this time was whether Emperors had the unilateral power to appoint church officials without approval from Rome. Gelasius I (#49), six centuries earlier, had articulated the revolutionary 'two powers' (or 'two swords') *Duo sunt* theory.

This being that the world is ruled by two chief powers: priestly powers culminating in the pope and royal power as wielded by the Emperor. The priestly powers, however, had more sway since they held the fate of the Emperor come the day of judgment. Was this the message that Coniulo intended to reinforce when he chose to be Gelasius II? This was the only time this name has been assumed.

In a similar vein, Alexander III (#171) and Sergius IV (#143) were elected during periods when the papacy was being coerced by secular leaders – the Holy Roman Emperor in the case of the former, and Crescentius III, the then ruler of Rome, in the case of the latter. Consequently, they may have chosen the names they did because both Alexander II (#157) and Sergius I (#84) were known for resisting interference from secular rulers.

On the other hand, when Desiderius was elected in 1087, he wanted to make peace with the Holy Roman Emperor Henry IV (1084-1105). He thus chose to be Victor III (#159). Victor II (#154) had been Henry's guardian, a trusted friend of his father's, and possibly even a relative. This is the one blatant example of a politically motivated papal name choice.

Romanus, the younger brother of Benedict VIII (#144), was a Tusculum. Though the Tusculums were still very much in charge of Rome, 'Romanus' wanted to reach out to the other Roman dynasties – in particular the Crescentiis. This was probably why he became John XIX (#145) – the last two popes named 'John' having been appointed by the Crescentiis.

The two remaining popes in this political category are Innocent VIII (#214) and his successor Alexander 'Rodrigo Borgia' VI (#215). Innocent was elected close to 70 years after the Great Western Schism [p. 60] had been successfully resolved. Nonetheless, it is believed that he took his name as a means of validating Innocent VII (#205) – a pope from the Roman obedience [i.e., branch] during the Schism. Innocent was the first pope to be elected in a conclave held at the newly built Sistine Chapel.

Rodrigo's uncle, Callistus 'Alfonso' III (#210), was born in Spain in 1378 – the same year that the Schism came into being. The Schism lasted 39 years. Alfonso studied and taught law before joining the Royal court in Aragón [Spain, but on the French border] sometime prior to 1416. Since the King of Aragón was one of the royals trying to resolve the Schism, Alfonso may have had some dealings with the parties involved. But there is no record of this.

Rodrigo was born in 1431 – 14 years after the Schism. It is possible that his doting uncle, who made him a cardinal, shared some insights with him as to what really happened, behind closed doors so to speak, during the Schism. Rodrigo chose to be Alexander VI. By doing so, he set out, unilaterally, to validate Alexander (V) – the antipope from the Pisan branch [p. 61]! But this did not alter Alexander (V's) standing vis-à-vis the Vatican.

Affinity with early church leaders and rapport with prior popes
Clement II (#150), Damasus II (#152) and Leo IX (#153), in addition to the two Silvesters mentioned earlier, all assumed their names to denote affinity with an early church leader – in each case the first pope of that name. Victor II (#154), who followed Leo IX, is also thought to have used the same rationale as is believed of Alexander II (#157) – two popes later. Another two popes later there was Urban II (#160), and two popes later again Callistus II (#163). Three popes later there was Lucius II (#167).

Harking back to the early church leaders seems to have been quite a trend during the 100 year period from 1045 to 1144 – with it having been most pronounced at the front-end. There appears to be a very good reason for this – viz. the indefensible machinations of the three-term Benedict IX (#146, #148 & #151). Note that Sylvester's and Clement's papacies occurred in between the three terms. Damasus and Leo came immediately after the third term. It was as if these popes wanted the church to return to the 'good old days.'

After Lucius, there was a 40 year gap before Clement III (#175), and then a significant gap before Clement VII (#220) and Leo X (#218). It is easy to rationalize the two Silvesters, Clement II, Damasus II and Leo IX. The other eight instances, however, are based on supposition – given the absence of any other evidence to clarify their choice of name. It is interesting that Clement I 'St. Clement of Rome' (#4), the first pope known to have postulated papal primacy, is the earliest pope invoked, while Leo I 'the Great' (#45) is the last. Linus, initially credited as being the first pope, has yet to be honored. It is, however, possible that as with Peter, his name too is considered sacrosanct.

Other than with Julius III (#222) and Clement IX (#239), who did indicate their rationale, the other nine instances in the rapport category have to be based on supposition. In two instances, viz. Clement IV (#184) and Gregory XI (#202), the desire to make peace with Rome may have been the motive. By the time the French Clement IV was elected, a pope had not resided in Rome for over five years due to factional unrest. Clement III (#175), 70 years earlier, had healed a five decade long rift with Rome that had permitted the papacy to return. Clement IV had hoped to achieve the same goal – but was foiled in the end.

Gregory XI, another Frenchman, was the last of the *bona fide* Avignon popes. He was committed from the start to returning the papacy to Rome – and to his credit did so. He most likely assumed that name because Gregory X (#185), Clement IV's successor, did succeed in going back to Rome. On the other hand, Clement VI (#199), the 4th Avignon pope, most likely assumed his name to show his rapport with the 1st Avignon pope, Clement V (#196).

Gregory X was elected while he was in Acre [Palestine] with the 9th Crusade. He probably chose his name to indicate his bonding with Gregory IX (#179) – an ardent supporter of the Crusades. Honorius III (#178) and Celestine V (#193) were considerably more pacific. It would appear that Honorius III, anxious to maintain amicable relationships with secular leaders, identified with Honorius II (#164), who had been successful in doing so. Celestine V, who had been a monk, may have assumed his name because Celestine IV (#180) was thought to have been a monk. Furthermore, the 'Celestines' had a reputation for scholarship.

It is also believed that Alexander IV (#182) could relate to Alexander III's (#171) assertiveness, while Gregory IX (#179) agreed with the authoritative leadership of Gregory VII (#158), and Urban III (#173) with the boldness of Urban II (#160) – the pope who launched the first Crusade in 1095.

Collocation from the past
Five decisive instances that fall into this category, e.g., Gregory XVI (#255) and Sixtus V, were described earlier, with the basis for Gregory XVI's choice of name providing the opening for this chapter. There is only one other verifiable instance that falls into this category, viz. Innocent X (#237). Though Innocent was born in Rome, his ancestors had moved to Rome in the late 15th century during the papacy of Innocent VIII (#214).

The other fifteen instances are all based on conjecture. The basis for the conjecture, in each instance, is summarized, pithily, below – the list ordered in alphabetical order of the names:

൫ Benedict XII (#198): probably for St. Benedict of Nursia (c. 489-c. 547), the pioneer of Christian monasticism, given that the pope-elect had been Cistercian monk. St. Benedict was also cited by Benedict XVI (#266) [p. 96].

൫ Benedict XV (#259): He and Benedict XIV (#248) had both been the Archbishop of Bologna.

൫ Celestine II (#166): Was a scholar like Celestine I (#43); Celestine I was believed to have corresponded with St. Ambrose (c. 338 – 397) and St. Augustine of Hippo (c. 354 – 430) – two bestriding intellectuals of the early Church.

൫ Eugene III (#168): He and Eugene I (#75) had both entered the church at an early age.

൫ Eugene IV (#208): He and Eugene III (#168) had both been monks.

൫ Gregory VIII (#174): He and Gregory I (#64) had both been monks.

൫ Gregory XII (#206): He and Gregory II (#89), in earlier times of their career, had spent time in Constantinople.

൫ Hadrian IV (#170): The only Englishman to date to become pope may have been acknowledging Hadrian I's (#96) efforts to strengthen Christianity in England during the late 8th century.

൫ Innocent VII (#205): He and Innocent V (#186) were both noted scholars.

൫ Innocent IX (#231): Like VII (above) and Innocent V he too was an expert in canon law.

൫ Lucius III (#172): Was born in c. 1097 and was made a cardinal by Innocent II (#165), on or before 1143. As a cardinal, he would have had considerable dealing with Lucius II (#167) who was pope from 1144 to 1145.

൫ Paschal II (#161): He and Paschal I (#99) were both monks – but it is also possible that he was born during Easter and chose this name because of that.

൫ Paul III (#221): Was born during Paul II's (#212) reign.

ℭℛ Urban VII (#229): Was legate to France while both Urban IV (#183) & V (#201) were French – and even VI (#203) had spent 20 years in Avignon [France].

ℭℛ Urban VIII (#236): He and Urban V (#201) both had doctorates in canon law; he and Urban VII (#229) had both held office in Bologna.

THE REGNAL NAMES

In the case of 50 of the 81 elemental names [p. 69], the Latinized papal regnal name [p. 15] is the same as the Anglicized 'popular' version of that name – or a very minor variant of it. 'Linus,' 'Anacletus'(/'Cletus'), 'Alexander,' 'Pius,' 'Victor,' "Felix,' 'Leo,' 'Agapetus'/'Agapitus,' 'Donus,' 'Conon,' 'Formosus' and 'Lando' all fall into this category.

Thus, there are 31 names where the regnal differs from the 'popular' name. These 31 names, in alphabetical order, with the regal name in parenthesis are as follows: Benedict (*Benedictus*), Boniface (*Bonifacius/Bonifatius*), Clement (*Clemens*), Celestine (*Coelestinus*), Constantine (*Constantinus*), Eleutherius (*Eleutherius*), Eugene (*Eugenius*), Eutychian (*Eutychianus*), Fabian (*Fabianus*), Gregory (*Gregorius*), Hadrian (*Hadrianus*), Hormisdas (*Hormisdus*), Innocent (*Innocentius*), John (*Ioannes*), John Paul (*Ioannes Paulus*), Julius (*Iulius*), Mark (*Marcus*), Martin (*Martinus*), Nicholas (*Nicholaus*), Paschal (*Paschalis*), Paul (*Paulus*), Peter (*Petrus*), Pontian (*Pontianus*), Sabinian (*Sabinianus*), Sixtus (*Xystus*), Soter (*Soterius*), Stephen (*Stephanus*), Theodore (*Theodorus*) Urban (*Urbanus*), Valentine (*Valentinus*) and Vitalian (*Vitalianus*).

The Latin for the ordinals, up to 24 just in case the next pope decides to be 'John,' are as follows:

I (*Primus*), II (*Secundus*), III (*Tertius*), IV (*Quartus*), V (*Quintus*), VI (*Sextus*), VII (*Septumus*), VIII (*Octavus*), IX (*Nonus*), X (*Decimus*), XI (*Undecimus*), XII (*Duodecimus*), XIII (*Tertius Decimus*), XIV (*Quartus Decimus*), XV (*Quintus Decimus*), XVI (*Sextus Decimus*), XVII (*Septimus Decimus*), XVIII (*Duodevicesimus*), XIX (*Undevicesimus*), XX (*Vicesimus*), XXI (*Vicesimus Primus*), XXII (*Vicesimus Secundus*), XXIII (*Vicesimus Tertius*), XXIV (*Vicesimus Quartus*).

It is customary to have *Papa* (pope) in front of the regnal name, and the pope's official title *Episcopus Romanus* (Bishop of Rome) after it. Thus,

Gregory XVI would be referred to as: *Papa Gregorius Sextus Decimus, Eposcopus Romanus. Magnus* for 'great' is used after the name of the three 'Greats.'

PAPAL NAMES IN COMMON SECULAR USAGE

The Gregorian calendar, Sistine Chapel and the Gregorian chant are quintessential examples, albeit with the last, credited to Gregory I 'the Great' (#64), now believed to be somewhat poetic. Per current thinking, the basis for these chants originated, mainly among the then Germanic tribes, about 100 years after Gregory. Eggs Benedict is not included in the above list since its association with a pope is even more tenuous.

Some, including Vatican expert Nino Lo Bello, have contended that the hollandaise sauce smothered breakfast favorite gets its name from Benedict XIII (#246), who liked to start off his day with eggs prepared as such. This, however, is hard to corroborate given that more worldly 'Benedicts,' from New York's financial sector, are also routinely credited with its creation.

But in deference to the pope, these financial Benedicts postdate him by nearly 150 years. On the other hand, Benedict, though from the powerful (and wealthy) Orsini family, and furthermore related to the noble Frangipani family via his mother, was a friar, from a young age, who shunned ostentation. So, there is a chance that this dish was a tad too rich for his tastes even by eighteenth century culinary standards. 'Eggs Benedict XVI,' with Rye Bread and sausage, is a recent and esoteric novelty inspired by the election of Benedict XVI (#266).

The Gregorian calendar, the basis for time in the West for the last 400 years, is now by far the most predominant calendar in the world. Considered to be secular (despite its origins), it has been the primary basis for world trade for at least the last two centuries. Its popularity and relevance has been further enhanced by the Web where it is the one calendar system that transcends national, cultural and religious differences. The Gregorian calendar was a refinement to the Julian calendar which had been introduced by Roman Emperor Julius Caesar in 46 BC. It is named after Gregory XIII (#227), whose papal bull *Inter gravissimas* on February 24, 1582 decreed the adoption of the new calendar starting on October 4th of that year. The Julian calendar was 10 days out of step by then.

APPENDIX A:
MEANINGS OF THE NAMES

Key:

▷ If no birth name is stated, the papal name is *assumed* to be the birth name.

▷ The meaning of the birth name is shown in column 4 → 'meaning'.

▷ All the papal names, with the exception of Peter, Sixtus and John Paul, first appeared as birth names. The derivations for Peter, Sixtus and John Paul are shown underneath their entry in column 2.

▷ 'First', 'Prev' and 'Next' columns refer to the first, previous and next occurrence of that papal name. Shading denotes consecutive use.

▷ Refer to the first occurrence of a papal name for its meaning using the sequence number (#) shown in column 5 → 'First'.

▷ Abbreviations: Ar: Aramaic, Ge: German, Gr: Greek, Hb: Hebrew, Lt: Latin, Ph: Phoenician.

▷ # - sequence number. Solid line denotes century splits. ? = uncertainty.

#	Papal Name	Birth Name →	Meaning	First	Prev	Next
1	St. Peter (Gr: 'rock')	Simon bar Jonah	Hb: to be heard			
2	St. Linus		Gr: flaxen haired; son of Apollo?			
3	St. Anacletus [also Cletus]	Cletus?	Gr: blameless			
4	St. Clement I [St. Clement of Rome]		Lt: gentle			150
5	St. Evaristus [also Aristus]		Gr: pleasing			
6	St. Alexander I		Gr: defender of men			157
7	St. Sixtus I (sixth) [also Xystus I]	Xystus <page 35>	Gr: shaved or polished			24
8	St. Telesphorus		Gr: accomplished			

#	Papal Name	Birth Name →	Meaning	First	Prev	Next
9	St. Hyginus		Gr: healthy			
10	St. Pius I		Lt: dutiful			211
11	St. Anicetus		Gr: unconquered			
12	St. Soter		Gr: savior			
13	St. Eleutherius [*also Eleutherus*]		Gr: frank?			
14	St. Victor I		Lt: champion			154
15	St. Zephyrinus		Gr: west wind			
16	St. Callistus I [*also Callixtus I*]		Gr: handsome			163
17	St. Urban I		Lt: city (born)			160
18	St. Pontian		Region in Greece?			
19	St. Anterus [*also Anteros*]		Greek god of love returned			
20	St. Fabian		Lt: bean grower			
21	St. Cornelius		Lt: horn (colored)			
22	St. Lucius I		Lt: bringer of light			167
23	St. Stephen I		Gr: crown			92
24	St. Sixtus II [*also Xystus II*]			7	7	44
25	St. Dionysius		Gr: god of wine			
26	St. Felix I		Lt: happy			48
27	St. Eutychian		Gr: fortunate			
28	St. Caius		Lt: rejoice			
29	St. Marcellinus		Dedicated to Mars, Roman god of war			
30	St. Marcellus I		See #29			223
31	St. Eusebius		Gr: devout			
32	St. Miltiades [*also Melchiades*]		Gr: red earth			
33	St. Silvester I [*also Sylvester I*]		Lt: woods, wooded			140

#	Papal Name	Birth Name →	Meaning	First	Prev	Next
34	St. Mark	Marcus	See #29			
35	St. Julius I		son of Jove (Jupiter)/ Lt: downy beard → youthful			217
36	Liberius		Lt: free			
37	St. Damasus I		Queen's kin or from Syria?			152
38	St. Siricius		From Syria?			
39	St. Anastasius I		Gr: resurrection			50
40	St. Innocent I	Innocentius	Lt: harmless			165
41	St. Zosimus		Lt: survivor			
42	St. Boniface I		Lt: fortunate			55
43	St. Celestine I		Lt: heavenly			166
44	St. Sixtus III [also Xystus III]			7	24	213
45	St. Leo I *the Great*		Lt: lion			80
46	St. Hilarius		Lt: joyful			
47	St. Simplicius		Lt: simple; (or he who is good?)			
48	St. Felix III			26	26	54
49	St. Gelasius I		Lt: bright; Gr: laughter			162
50	Anastasius II			39	39	121
51	St. Symmachus		Hb: joy?			
52	St. Hormisdas		Persian: one of the Magi in Syrian			
53	St. John I		Hb: God is gracious			56
54	St. Felix IV			26	48	
55	Boniface II			42	42	66
56	John II	Mercurius	Mercury; Roman messenger god	53	53	61

#	Papal Name	Birth Name →	Meaning	First	Prev	Next
57	St. Agapetus I [*also Agapitus I*]		Gk: beloved			130
58	St. Silverius		Lt: woods, forest?			
59	Vigilius		Lt: vigilant			
60	Pelagius I		Lt: from or across the sea			63
61	John III	Catelinus	Gr: pure; Lt: wise?	53	56	72
62	Benedict I		Lt: blessed			81
63	Pelagius II			60	60	
64	St. Gregory I *the Great*		Gr: watchful/ vigilant			89
65	Sabinian		From Italian region of Sabina or possibly vine grower			
66	Boniface III			42	55	67
67	St. Boniface IV			42	66	69
68	St. Deusdedit [*also Adeodatus I*]		Lt: God given			
69	Boniface V			42	67	113
70	Honorius I		Lt: honorable			164
71	Severinus		Lt: firm/stern			
72	John IV			53	61	82
73	Theodore I		Gr: God's gift			116
74	St. Martin I		See #29			190
75	St. Eugene I		Gr: well born			100
76	St. Vitalian		Lt: full of life			
77	Adeodatus (II)		See #68			
78	Donus		Lt: gift from God (or Lordly?)			
79	St. Agatho		Gr: good			
80	St. Leo II			45	45	97
81	St. Benedict II			62	62	105

#	Papal Name	Birth Name →	Meaning	First	Prev	Next
82	John V			53	72	85
83	Conon		little horse since it may be Thracian?; Gr: for cone?			
84	St. Sergius I		Lt: servant (of Christ)?			103
85	John VI			53	82	86
86	John VII			53	85	108
87	Sisinnius		Lt: curly (golden) hair?			
88	Constantine		Lt: constant, steadfast			
89	St. Gregory II			64	64	90
90	St. Gregory III			64	89	102
91	St. Zacharias [*also Zachary*]		Hb: God has remembered			
92	Stephen (II)			23	23	93
93	Stephen II (III)			23	92	95
94	St. Paul I		Lt: humble or small			212
95	Stephen III (IV)			23	93	98
96	Hadrian I [*also Adrian I*]		From Hadria, Northern Italy			107
97	St. Leo III			45	80	104
98	Stephen IV (V)			23	95	111
99	St. Paschal I		Lt: relating to Easter			161
100	Eugene II			75	75	168
101	Valentine		Lt: strong, vigorous, healthy			
102	Gregory IV			64	90	139
103	Sergius II			84	84	120
104	St. Leo IV			45	97	119
105	Benedict III			62	81	118
106	St. Nicholas I *the Great*		Gr: victory of the people			156

#	Papal Name	Birth Name →	Meaning	First	Prev	Next
107	Hadrian II [*also Adrian II*]			96	96	110
108	John VIII			53	86	117
109	Marinus I [*also Martin II*]		Lt: of the sea			129
110	St. Hadrian III [*also St. Adrian III*]			96	107	170
111	Stephen V (VI)			23	98	114
112	Formosus		Lt: beautiful			
113	Boniface VI			42	69	194
114	Stephen VI (VII)			23	111	125
115	Romanus		Lt: Roman			
116	Theodore II			73	73	
117	John IX			53	108	123
118	Benedict IV			62	105	133
119	Leo V			45	104	124
120	Sergius III			84	103	143
121	Anastasius III			39	50	169
122	Lando		Ge: of the land			
123	John X			53	117	126
124	Leo VI			45	119	127
125	Stephen VII (VIII)			23	114	128
126	John XI			53	123	131
127	Leo VII			45	124	132
128	Stephen VIII (IX)			23	125	155
129	Marinus II [*also Martin III*]			109	109	
130	Agapetus II [*also Agapitus II*]			57	57	
131	John XII ("boy pope")	Octavian	Lt: eight	53	126	134
132	Leo VIII			45	127	153
133	Benedict V			62	118	135
134	John XIII			53	131	137
135	Benedict VI			62	133	136

#	Papal Name	Birth Name →	Meaning	First	Prev	Next
136	Benedict VII			62	135	144
137	John XIV	Pietro Canepanova	It: Peter → Rock	53	134	*138*
138	John XV			53	*137*	141
139	Gregory V	Bruno of Carinthia	Ge: brown	64	102	149
140	Silvester II [*also Sylvester II*]	Gerbert d'Aurillac	Ge: glittering spear	33	33	147
141	John XVII	John Sicco		53	138	142
142	John XVIII (XIX)	Giovanni (John) Fasanus		53	141	145
143	Sergius IV	Pietro '*Bucca Porci*' [pig's snout]	It: Peter → Rock	84	120	
144	Benedict VIII	Theophylact(us) II – Tusculum family	Gr: protected by God	62	136	146
145	John XIX	Romanus – Tusculum family	See #115	53	142	188
146	Benedict IX – 1st term	Theophylact(us) III – Tusculum family	See #144	62	144	148
147	Silvester III [*also Sylvester III*]	John, Bishop of Sabina	See #53	33	140	
148	Benedict IX – 2nd term	Theophylact(us) III	Same pope as #146	62	146	151
149	Gregory VI	John Gratian	See #53	64	139	158
150	Clement II	Suidger, Bishop of Bamberg	own spear? soldier?	4	4	175
151	Benedict IX – 3rd term	Theophylact(us) III	Same pope as #146	62	148	195
152	Damasus II	Poppo, Bishop of Brixen	Lt: poppy flower?	37	37	
153	St. Leo IX	Bruno, Bishop of Toul	See #139	45	132	218
154	Victor II	Gebhard, Bishop of Eichstätt	Ge: gift of bravery/strength	14	14	159

#	Papal Name	Birth Name →	Meaning	First	Prev	Next
155	Stephen IX (X)	Frederick of Lorraine	Ge: peaceful ruler	23	128	
156	Nicholas II	Gérard of Burgundy	Ge: brave spear carrier	106	106	189
157	Alexander II	Anselm da Baggio	Ge: God's helmet	6	6	171
158	St. Gregory VII	Hildebrand	Ge: battle sword	64	149	174
159	Victor III	born: Daufari *then* Desiderius (Desiderio)	pigeon(/dove) ? *then* Lt: yearning; desire	14	154	
160	Urban II	Odo (Otho) of Lagery	Ge: wealthy	17	17	173
161	Paschal II	Rainerius	Ge: wise warrior?	99	99	
162	Gelasius II	Giovanni Coniulo	John; See #53	49	49	
163	Callistus II [*also Callixtus II*]	Guido of Vienne	Fr: leader Ge: warrior; It: wood	16	16	210
164	Honorius II	Lamberto Scannabecchi	Lt: wealthy in land; brilliant	70	70	178
165	Innocent II	Gregorio Papareschi	Gregory; See #64	40	40	177
166	Celestine II	Guido of Città di Castello	See #163	43	43	176
167	Lucius II	Gherardo Caccianemici dal Orso	Gerard; See #156	22	22	172
168	Eugene III	Bernardo dei Paganelli	Ge: brave as a bear	75	100	208
169	Anastasius IV	Corrado della Suburra	Conrad; Ge: brave advisor	39	121	
170	Hadrian IV [*also Adrian IV*]	Nicholas Breakspear	See #106	96	110	187
171	Alexander III	Olando Bandinelli	Lt: famed throughout the land; (gold coast?)	6	157	182
172	Lucius III	Ubaldo Allucingoli	It: peace of mind	22	167	

#	Papal Name	Birth Name →	Meaning	First	Prev	Next
173	Urban III	Umberto Crivelli	It/Ge: famous warrior	17	160	183
174	Gregory VIII	Alberto de Morra	Ge: noble and famous	64	158	179
175	Clement III	Paulino Scolari	Paul; See #94	4	150	184
176	Celestine III	Giacinto Bobo (Orsini)	It: Hyacinth – Greek god & flower	43	166	180
177	Innocent III	Lotario de' Conti di Segni	Luther; Ge: famous warrior/army /people	40	165	181
178	Honorius III	Cencio Savelli	Vincent; conqueror	70	164	191
179	Gregory IX	Ugolino de' Conti di Segni	Italian form of Hugo; thinker	64	174	185
180	Celestine IV	Goffredo da Castiglione	Godfrey; Ge: God's peace	43	176	193
181	Innocent IV	Sinibaldo Fieschi	Sinbad; sparkling prince	40	177	186
182	Alexander IV	Rinaldo de' Conti di Segni	Reginald; Lt: wise ruler	6	171	215
183	Urban IV	Jacques Pantaléon	Jacob; Hb: supplant; (held by the heel)	17	173	201
184	Clement IV	Gui Faucoi	Guy; Ge: warrior; guide; wood	4	175	196
185	Gregory X	Tebaldo Visconti	Theobald; people's prince	64	179	202
186	Innocent V	Pierre de Tarentaise	Peter; See #1	40	181	200
187	Hadrian V [*also Adrian V*]	Ottobuono de' Fieschi	Good 8th born? Born in October?	96	170	219
188	John XXI	Pedro Julião (Hispano)	Peter; See #1	53	145	197

#	Papal Name	Birth Name →	Meaning	First	Prev	Next
189	Nicholas III	Giovanni Gaetano – Orsini family	John; See #53	106	156	192
190	Martin IV	Simon de Brion	See #1	74	74	207
191	Honorius IV	Giacomo Savelli	Jacob; See #183	70	178	
192	Nicholas IV	Girolamo Masci	It: holy name	106	189	209
193	St. Celestine V	Pietro Angelerio (Pietro del Morrone)	Peter; See #1	43	180	
194	Boniface VIII	Benedetto Caetani	Benedict; See #62	42	113	204
195	Benedict XI	Nicholas Boccasino	See #106	62	151	198
196	Clement V	Bertrand de Goth	Bertram; bright raven	4	184	199
197	John XXII	Jacques Duèze (d'Euse)	Jacob; See #183	53	188	262
198	Benedict XII	Jacques Fournier	Jacob; See #183	62	195	246
199	Clement VI	Pierre Roger	Peter; See #1	4	196	220
200	Innocent VI	Étienne Aubert	Stephen; See #23	40	186	205
201	Urban V	Guillaume de Grimoard	William; Ge: gold helmet; protected	17	183	203
202	Gregory XI	Pierre Roger de Beaufort	Peter; See #1	64	185	206
203	Urban VI	Bartolomeo Prignano	Bartholomew; Ar: son of a farmer	17	201	229
204	Boniface IX	Pietro Tomacelli	Peter; See #1	42	194	
205	Innocent VII	Cosimo Gentile de' Migliorati	Cosmo; Ge/It: order; beauty; harmony	40	200	214
206	Gregory XII	Angelo Correr (Corrario)	Angel; Ge: messenger of God	64	202	227
207	Martin V	Odo (Oddone) Colonna	Otto; Ge: wealthy	74	190	

#	Papal Name	Birth Name →	Meaning	First	Prev	Next
208	Eugene IV	Gabriele Condulmer	He: able bodied man of God	75	168	
209	Nicholas V	Tommaso Parentucelli	Thomas; Ar: twin	106	192	
210	Callistus III [also Callixtus III]	Alfonso de Borja (Borgia)	Alphonse; Ge: ready for battle	16	163	
211	Pius II	Enea Silvio Piccolomini	Aeneas; Lt: praise	10	10	216
212	Paul II	Pietro Barbo	Peter; See #1	94	94	221
213	Sixtus IV	Francesco della Rovere	Lt: from France; [free man?]	7	44	228
214	Innocent VIII	Giovanni Battista Cibò	John; See #53	40	205	231
215	Alexander VI	Rodrigo de Borja (Borgia)	Roderick; Ge: famous (powerful) ruler	6	182	238
216	Pius III	Francesco Todeschini Piccolomini	See #213	10	211	225
217	Julius II "Warrior Pope"	Giuliano della Rovere	It: Julius; See #35	35	35	222
218	Leo X	Giovanni di Lorenzo de' Medici	John; See #53	45	153	233
219	Hadrian VI [also Adrian VI]	Adrian Florensz Dedal (Boeyens)	See #96	96	187	
220	Clement VII	Giulio di Giuliano de' Medici	It: Julius (as Giuliano); See #35	4	199	232
221	Paul III	Alessandro Farnese	Alexander ; See #6	94	212	224
222	Julius III	Giovanni Maria Ciocchi del Monte	John; See #53	35	217	
223	Marcellus II	Marcello Cervini degli Spannochi	Marcellus; See #30	30	30	

#	Papal Name	Birth Name →	Meaning	First	Prev	Next
224	Paul IV	Giovanni Pietro Carafa	John; See #53	94	221	234
225	Pius IV	Giovanni (Gian) Angelo de Medici	John; See #53	10	216	226
226	St. Pius V	Antonio/ Michele Ghislieri	Anthony; invaluable/ Hb: resembles God	10	225	251
227	Gregory XIII	Ugo Boncompagni	Hugo; Ge: bright in spirit and insight	64	206	230
228	Sixtus V	Felice Peretti	Felix; See #26	7	213	
229	Urban VII	Giovan(ni) (Giam) Battista Castagna	John; See #53	17	203	236
230	Gregory XIV	Niccolò Sfondrati	Nicholas; See #106	64	227	235
231	Innocent IX	Giovanni Antonio Facchinetti	John; See #53	40	214	237
232	Clement VIII	Ippolito Aldobrandini	Hippolyte; Ge: free, galloping horse	4	220	239
233	Leo XI	Alessandro Ottaviano de' Medici	Alexander ; See #6	45	218	253
234	Paul V	Camillo Borghese	temple attendant	94	224	263
235	Gregory XV	Alessandro Ludovisi	Alexander ; See #6	64	230	255
236	Urban VIII	Maffeo Barberini	Matthew; He: gift of God	17	229	
237	Innocent X	Giovanni/Gian Battista Pamphilj (Pamfili)	John; See #53	40	231	241
238	Alexander VII	Fabio Chigi	(little) Fabian; See # 20	6	215	242
239	Clement IX	Giulio Rospigliosi	See #220	4	232	240

#	Papal Name	Birth Name →	Meaning	First	Prev	Next
240	Clement X	Emilio Bonaventura Altieri	Emil; Lt: eager	4	239	244
241	Innocent XI	Benedetto Odescalchi	Benedict; See #62	40	237	243
242	Alexander VIII	Pietro Vito Ottoboni	Peter; See #1	6	238	
243	Innocent XII	Antonio Pignatelli	Anthony; See #226	40	241	245
244	Clement XI	Giovanni Francesco Albani	John; See #53	4	240	247
245	Innocent XIII	Michelangelo dei Conti	It: messenger (angel) who resembles God	40	243	
246	Benedict XIII	Pietro Francesco Orsini	Peter; See #1	62	198	248
247	Clement XII	Lorenzo Corsini	Lt: from Laurentum (ancient Roman city)	4	244	249
248	Benedict XIV	Prospero Lorenzo Lambertini	Lt: fortunate	62	246	259
249	Clement XIII	Carlo della Torre di Rezzonico	Charles; Ge : strong/free man	4	247	250
250	Clement XIV	Giovanni Vincenzo Antonio Ganganelli	John; See #53	4	249	
251	Pius VI	Giovanni Angelo Braschi	John; See #53	10	226	252
252	Pius VII	Barnabà Niccolò Maria Luigi Chiaramonti	Barnabas; Hb: son of a prophet	10	251	254
253	Leo XII	Annibale Francesco Clemente Melchiore Girolamo Nicola della Genga	Hannibal; Ph: by the grace of the Lord; orgracious and beautiful?	45	233	257

#	Papal Name	Birth Name →	Meaning	First	Prev	Next
254	Pius VIII	Francesco Saverio Castiglioni	See #213	10	252	256
255	Gregory XVI	Bartolomeo Alberto Cappellari	See #203	64	235	
256	Pius IX	Giovanni Maria Mastai-Ferretti	John; See #53	10	254	258
257	Leo XIII	Gioacchino Vincenzo Raffaele Luigi Pecci	Joachim; Hb: established by God	45	253	
258	St. Pius X	Giuseppe Melchiorre Sarto	Joseph; Hb: the Lord will add	10	256	260
259	Benedict XV	Giacomo Paolo Giovanni Battista della Chiesa	Jacob; See #183	62	248	266
260	Pius XI	Ambrogio Damiano Achille Ratti	Ambrose; Gr: immortal	10	258	261
261	Pius XII	Eugenio Maria Giuseppe Giovanni Pacelli	Eugene; See #75	10	260	
262	John XXIII	Angelo Giuseppe Roncalli	See #206	53	197	
263	Paul VI	Giovanni Battista Enrico Antonio Maria Montini	John; See #53	94	234	
264	John Paul I (For #262 & #263)	Albino Luciani	Lt: white; from Alba (Scotland)?			265
265	John Paul II	Karol Józef Wojtyła	Charles; See #249	264	264	
266	Benedict XVI	Joseph Alois Ratzinger	See #258	62	259	

APPENDIX B:
MASTER LIST OF POPES
IN CHRONOLOGICAL ORDER

Notes:

▶ 266, 265, 264 or 263: This list, the basis for all the statistics quoted in this book (unless otherwise stated), contains 266 popes – up to and including Pope Benedict XVI (#266), who was elected April 2005. The current Vatican list has one less pope – *viz.* the original Stephen II (#92; March 752) who died 4 days after being elected. This Stephen, however, did appear in Vatican lists till 1961. He also appears in the papal list maintained by Wikipedia, the increasingly popular online encyclopedia. He is thus included in this list for completeness. The three separate terms of Benedict IX (#146, #148 & #151) are also listed separately, rather than as a single, grouped entry. Thus the differences in the numbers used in various lists are due to:

266 = includes original Stephen II (#92) and Benedict IX's 3 terms.

265 = without the original Stephen II but with 3 entries for Benedict IX.

264 = with the original Stephen II but with Benedict IX listed just once.

263 = without the original Stephen II and Benedict IX listed once.

▶ The start and end dates for papacies tend to be the most inclusive, i.e., the longest possible. The scope of this book limits the option of listing multiple alternate dates when there are deferring opinions about the dates. The start date in general refers to when the pope was elected (or received Imperial approval) rather than the date when the pope was consecrated.

▶ The lengths of the papacies, though probably the most accurate to-date, are still approximations in the main. They were calculated using fixed 30 day months with no rounding up of the months; i.e., months shown represent completed months. Thus a papacy whose duration was 4 years, 10 months and 23 days will be shown as 4y 10m.

▶ # - sequence number. ~ = approximately. ? = uncertainty. c. = circa; about. solid line denotes century splits; shading denotes consecutive use of the same name.

▶ Abbreviations: y – years, m – months, d – days, w – weeks

#	Papal Name	Start of reign	End of reign	Length	From
1	St. Peter	c. 42/57	c. 64/67	~25y	Holy Land
2	St. Linus	c. 64/67	c. 76/79	~12y	Italy
3	St. Anacletus	c. 76/79	c. 88/92	~12y	Greece
4	St. Clement I	c. 88/92	c. 97/101	~9y	Italy?
5	St. Evaristus	c. 97/101	c. 105/109	~9y	Greece?
6	St. Alexander I	c. 105/109	c. 115/116	~11y	Italy?
7	St. Sixtus I	c. 115/116	c. 125/128	~10y	Italy?
8	St. Telesphorus	c. 125/128	c. 136/138	~11y	Greece?
9	St. Hyginus	c. 136/138	c. 140/142	~4y	Greece
10	St. Pius I	c. 140/142	c. 154/155	~15y	Italy?
11	St. Anicetus	c. 154/155	c. 166/167	~11y	Syria
12	St. Soter	c. 166/167	c. 174/175	~9y	Italy
13	St. Eleutherius	c. 174/175	c. 189	~15y	Balkans
14	St. Victor I	189	198/199	~10y	N. Africa
15	St. Zephyrinus	199	217	~18y	Italy
16	St. Callistus I	217	222/223	~5y	Greece?
17	St. Urban I	222/223	230	~8y 11m	Italy
18	St. Pontian	21 July 230	28 Sep 235	5y 2m	Italy
19	St. Anterus	21 Nov 235	3 Jan 236	43 days	Greece?
20	St. Fabian	10 Jan 236	20 Jan 250	14y	Italy
21	St. Cornelius	Mar/Apr 251	June 253	~2y 3m	Italy
22	St. Lucius I	25 June 253	5 Mar 254	9m	Italy
23	St. Stephen I	12 May 254	2 Aug 257	3y 3m	Italy
24	St. Sixtus II	30/31 Aug 257	6 Aug 258	11m	Greece
25	St. Dionysius	22 July 260	26 Dec 268	8y 5m	Greece?
26	St. Felix I	5 Jan 269	30 Dec 274	6y	Italy
27	St. Eutychian	4 Jan 275	7 Dec 283	8y 11m	Italy
28	St. Caius	17 Dec 283	22 Apr 296	12y 4m	Croatia
29	St. Marcellinus	30 June 296	304	~8y	Italy
30	St. Marcellus I	~306/308	~308/309	11m	Italy
31	St. Eusebius	18 Apr (310?)	21 Oct (310?)	6m	Greece?
32	St. Miltiades	2 July 311	10 Jan 314	2y 6m	Italy
33	St. Silvester I	31 Jan 314	31 Dec 335	21y 11m	Italy

#	Papal Name	Start of reign	End of reign	Length	From
34	St. Mark	18 Jan 336	7 Oct 336	8m 20d	Italy
35	St. Julius I	6 Feb 337	12 Apr 352	15y 2m	Italy
36	Liberius	22 May 352	24 Sep 366	14y 4m	Italy
37	St. Damasus I	1 Oct 366	11 Dec 384	18y 2m	Portugal
38	St. Siricius	Dec 384	26 Nov 399	14y 11m	Italy
39	St. Anastasius I	27 Nov 399	19 Dec 401	2y 22d	Italy
40	St. Innocent I	22 Dec 401	12 Mar 417	15y 3m	Italy
41	St. Zosimus	18 Mar 417	26 Dec 418	1y 9m	Greece?
42	St. Boniface I	29 Dec 418	4 Sep 422	3y 8m	Italy
43	St. Celestine I	10 Sep 422	27 Jul 432	9y 10m	Italy
44	St. Sixtus III	31 July 432	19 Aug 440	8y 19d	Italy
45	St. Leo I *the Great*	29 Sep 440	10 Nov 461	21y 42d	Italy
46	St. Hilarius	19 Nov 461	29 Feb 468	6y 3m	Italy
47	St. Simplicius	3 Mar 468	10 Mar 483	15y 7d	Italy
48	St. Felix III	13 Mar 483	1 Mar 492	9y	Italy
49	St. Gelasius I	1 Mar 492	21 Nov 496	4y 8m	Italy
50	Anastasius II	24 Nov 496	19 Nov 498	2y	Italy
51	St. Symmachus	22 Nov 498	19 July 514	15y 8m	Italy
52	St. Hormisdas	20 July 514	6 Aug 523	9y 17d	Italy
53	St. John I	13 Aug 523	18 May 526	2y 9m	Italy
54	St. Felix IV	12 Jul 526	22 Sep 530	4y 2m	Italy
55	Boniface II	22 Sep 530	17 Oct 532	2y 25d	Italy
56	John II	2 Jan 533	8 May 535	2y 4m	Italy
57	St. Agapetus I	13 May 535	22 Apr 536	11m	Italy
58	St. Silverius	8 June 536	11 Nov 537	1y 5m	Italy
59	Vigilius	29 Mar 537	7 Jun 555	18y 2m	Italy
60	Pelagius I	16 Apr 556	4 Mar 561	4y 10m	Italy
61	John III	17 July 561	13 July 574	13y	Italy
62	Benedict I	2 June 575	30 July 579	4y 1m	Italy
63	Pelagius II	Aug 579	7 Feb 590	10y 6m	Italy
64	St. Gregory I *the Great*	3 Sep 590	12 Mar 604	13y 6m	Italy

#	Papal Name	Start of reign	End of reign	Length	From
65	Sabinian	13 Sep 604	22 Feb 606	1y 5m	Italy
66	Boniface III	19 Feb 607	12 Nov 607	8m 3w	Italy
67	St. Boniface IV	15 Sep 608	8 May 615	6y 8m	Italy
68	St. Deusdedit	19 Oct 615	8 Nov 618	3y 19d	Italy
69	Boniface V	23 Dec 619	25 Oct 625	5y 10m	Italy
70	Honorius I	27 Oct 625	12 Oct 638	13y	Italy
71	Severinus	28 May 640	2 Aug 640	2m 5d	Italy
72	John IV	24 Dec 640	12 Oct 642	1 y 9m	Croatia
73	Theodore I	24 Nov 642	14 May 649	6y 5m	Palestine
74	St. Martin I	5 July 649	10 Aug 654	5y 36d	Italy
75	St. Eugene I	10 Aug 654	2 Jun 657	2y 10m	Italy
76	St. Vitalian	30 July 657	27 Jan 672	14y 6m	Italy
77	Adeodatus (II)	11 Apr 672	17 Jun 676	4y 2m	Italy
78	Donus	2 Nov 676	11 Apr 678	1y 5m	Italy
79	St. Agatho	27 June 678	10 Jan 681	2y 6m	Italy
80	St. Leo II	17 Aug 682	3 July 683	10m 20d	Italy
81	St. Benedict II	26 June 684	8 May 685	10m 16d	Italy
82	John V	23 July 685	2 Aug 686	1y 10d	Syria
83	Conon	21 Oct 686	21 Sep 687	11m	Balkans
84	St. Sergius I	15 Dec 687	9 Sep 701	13y 9m	Italy
85	John VI	30 Oct 701	11 Jan 705	3y 2m	Greece
86	John VII	1 Mar 705	18 Oct 707	2y 7m	Greece
87	Sisinnius	15 Jan 708	4 Feb 708	20 days	Syria
88	Constantine	25 Mar 708	9 Apr 715	7y	Syria
89	St. Gregory II	19 May 715	11 Feb 731	15y 9m	Italy
90	St. Gregory III	18 Mar 731	28 Nov 741	10y 8m	Syria
91	St. Zacharias	3 Dec 741	15 Mar 752	10y 3m	Italy
92	Stephen (II)	23 Mar 752	26 Mar 752	4 days	Italy?
93	Stephen II (III)	26 Mar 752	26 Apr 757	5y 1m	Italy
94	St. Paul I	29 May 757	28 June 767	10y 1m	Italy
95	Stephen III (IV)	7 Aug 768	24 Jan 772	3y 5m	Italy
96	Hadrian I	1 Feb 772	25 Dec 795	23y 10m	Italy
97	St. Leo III	26 Dec 795	12 June 816	20y 5m	Italy

#	Papal Name	Start of reign	End of reign	Length	From
98	Stephen IV (V)	22 June 816	24 Jan 817	7m 2d	Italy
99	St. Paschal I	24 Jan 817	11 Feb 824	7y	Italy
100	Eugene II	June 824	Aug 827	~3y 1m	Italy
101	Valentine	Aug 827	Sep 827	~1m	Italy
102	Gregory IV	late 827	25 Jan 844	~16y	Italy
103	Sergius II	Jan 844	27 Jan 847	3y	Italy
104	St. Leo IV	10 Apr 847	17 Jul 855	8y 3m	Italy
105	Benedict III	29 Sep 855	17 Apr 858	2y 6m	Italy
106	St. Nicholas I the Great	24 Apr 858	13 Nov 867	9y 6m	Italy
107	Hadrian II	14 Dec 867	Nov/Dec 872	5y	Italy
108	John VIII	14 Dec 872	16 Dec 882	10y 2d	Italy
109	Marinus I	16 Dec 882	15 May 884	1y 5m	Italy
110	St. Hadrian III	17 May 884	mid-Sep 885	1y 4m	Italy
111	Stephen V (VI)	late-Sep 885	14 Sep 891	6y	Italy
112	Formosus	6 Oct 891	4 Apr 896	4y 6m	Italy
113	Boniface VI	Apr 896	Apr 896	15 days	Italy
114	Stephen VI (VII)	May 896	Aug 897	1y 2m	Italy
115	Romanus	Aug 897	Nov 897	~3m	Italy
116	Theodore II	Nov 897	Nov(/Dec) 897	20 days	Italy
117	John IX	Jan 898	Jan 900	~2y	Italy
118	Benedict IV	May/June 900	Aug 903	~3y 3m	Italy
119	Leo V	Aug 903	Sep 903	~2m	Italy?
120	Sergius III	29 Jan 904	14 Apr 911	7y 2m	Italy
121	Anastasius III	June 911	Aug 913	~2y 1m	Italy
122	Lando	Aug 913	Mar 914	6m 11d	Italy
123	John X	Mar/Apr 914	May 928	~14y	Italy
124	Leo VI	May 928	Dec 928	~6m	Italy
125	Stephen VII (VIII)	Dec 928	Feb 931	~2y 2m	Italy
126	John XI	Feb/Mar 931	Dec 935/Jan 936	~4y 9m	Italy
127	Leo VII	3 Jan 936	13 July 939	3y 6m	Italy

#	Papal Name	Start of reign	End of reign	Length	From
128	Stephen VIII (IX)	14 July 939	late-Oct 942	~3y 3m	Italy
129	Marinus II	30 Oct 942	early-May 946	~3y 6m	Italy
130	Agapetus II	10 My 946	Dec 955	~9y 7m	Italy
131	John XII	16 Dec 955	14 May 964	8y 5m	Italy
132	Leo VIII	4 Dec 963	1 Mar 965	1y 2m	Italy
133	Benedict V	22 May 964	23 June 964	32 days	Italy
134	John XIII	1 Oct 965	6 Sep 972	6y 11m	Italy
135	Benedict VI	19 Jan 973	July 974	~1y 5m	Italy
136	Benedict VII	Oct 974	10 July 983	~8y 9m	Italy
137	John XIV	Dec 983	20 Aug 984	~8m	Italy
138	John XV	mid-Aug 985	Mar 996	~10y 7m	Italy
139	Gregory V	3 May 996	18 Feb 999	2y 9m	Germany
140	Silvester II	2 Apr 999	12 May 1003	4y 1m	France
141	John XVII	16 May 1003	6 Nov 1003	5m 25d	Italy
142	John XVIII (XIX)	25 Dec 1003	June/July 1009	~5y 6m	Italy
143	Sergius IV	31 July 1009	12 May 1012	2y 9m	Italy
144	Benedict VIII	17 May 1012	9 Apr 1024	11y 11m	Italy
145	John XIX	19 Apr 1024	20 Oct 1032	8y 6m	Italy
146	Benedict IX – 1st term	21 Oct 1032	15 Sep 1044	~11y 11m	Italy
147	Silvester III	20 Jan 1045	10 Mar 1045	49 days	Italy
148	Benedict IX – 2nd term	10 Mar 1045	1 May 1045	52 days	Italy
149	Gregory VI	1 May 1045	20 Dec 1046	1 y 7m	Italy
150	Clement II	24 Dec 1046	9 Oct 1047	9m 19d	Germany
151	Benedict IX – 3rd term	8 Nov 1047	16 July 1048	8m 11d	Italy
152	Damasus II	17 July 1048	9 Aug 1048	23 days	Germany
153	St. Leo IX	12 Feb 1049	19 Apr 1054	5y 2m	Germany
154	Victor II	13 Apr 1055	28 July 1057	2y 3m	Germany
155	Stephen IX (X)	2 Aug 1057	29 Mar 1058	7m 29d	France
156	Nicholas II	6 Dec 1058	27 July 1061	2y 7m	France

#	Papal Name	Start of reign	End of reign	Length	From
157	Alexander II	30 Sep 1061	21 Apr 1073	11y 6m	Italy
158	St. Gregory VII	22 Apr 1073	25 May 1085	12y 1m	Italy
159	Victor III	9 May 1087	16 Sep 1087	4m 10d	Italy
160	Urban II	12 Mar 1088	29 July 1099	11y 4m	France
161	Paschal II	13 Aug 1099	21 Jan 1118	18y 5m	Italy
162	Gelasius II	24 Jan 1118	29 Jan 1119	1y 5d	Italy
163	Callistus II	2 Feb 1119	14 Dec 1124	5y 10m	France
164	Honorius II	21 Dec 1124	13 Feb 1130	5y 1m	Italy
165	Innocent II	14 Feb 1130	24 Sep 1143	13y 7m	Italy
166	Celestine II	26 Sep 1143	8 Mar 1144	5m 13d	Italy
167	Lucius II	12 March 1144	15 Feb 1145	11m	Italy
168	Eugene III	15 Feb 1145	8 July 1153	8y 4m	Italy
169	Anastasius IV	8 July 1153	3 Dec 1154	1y 4m	Italy
170	Hadrian IV	4 Dec 1154	1 Sep 1159	4y 9m	England
171	Alexander III	7 Sep 1159	30 Aug 1181	21y 11m	Italy
172	Lucius III	1 Sep 1181	25 Nov 1185	4y 2m	Italy
173	Urban III	25 Nov 1185	20 Oct 1187	1y 10m	Italy
174	Gregory VIII	21 Oct 1187	17 Dec 1187	57 days	Italy
175	Clement III	19 Dec 1187	late-Mar 1191	3y 3m	Italy
176	Celestine III	14 Apr 1191	8 Jan 1198	6y 9m	Italy
177	Innocent III	8 Jan 1198	16 July 1216	18y 6m	Italy
178	Honorius III	18 July 1216	18 Mar 1227	10y 8m	Italy
179	Gregory IX	19 Mar 1227	22 Aug 1241	14y 5m	Italy
180	Celestine IV	25 Oct 1241	10 Nov 1241	16 days	Italy
181	Innocent IV	25 June 1243	7 Dec 1254	11y 5m	Italy
182	Alexander IV	12 Dec 1254	25 May 1261	6y 5m	Italy
183	Urban IV	29 Aug 1261	2 Oct 1264	3y 1m	France
184	Clement IV	5 Feb 1265	29 Nov 1268	3y 9m	France
185	Gregory X	1 Sep 1271	10 Jan 1276	4y 4m	Italy
186	Innocent V	21 Jan 1276	22 June 1276	5m	France
187	Hadrian V	11 July 1276	18 Aug 1276	38 days	Italy

#	Papal Name	Start of reign	End of reign	Length	From
188	John XXI	8 Sep 1276	20 May 1277	8m 12d	Portugal
189	Nicholas III	25 Nov 1277	22 Aug 1280	2y 9m	Italy
190	Martin IV	22 Feb 1281	28 Mar 1285	4y 1m	France
191	Honorius IV	2 Apr 1285	3 Apr 1287	2y	Italy
192	Nicholas IV	22 Feb 1288	4 Apr 1292	4y 1m	Italy
193	St. Celestine V	5 July 1294	13 Dec 1294	5m 8d	Italy
194	Boniface VIII	24 Dec 1294	11 Oct 1303	8y 9m	Italy
195	Benedict XI	22 Oct 1303	7 July 1304	8m	Italy
196	Clement V	5 June 1305	20 Apr 1314	8y 10m	France
197	John XXII	7 Aug 1316	4 Dec 1334	18y 4m	France
198	Benedict XII	20 Dec 1334	25 Apr 1342	7y 4m	France
199	Clement VI	7 May 1342	6 Dec 1352	10y 7m	France
200	Innocent VI	18 Dec 1352	12 Sep 1362	9y 9m	France
201	Urban V	28 Sep 1362	19 Dec 1370	8y 2m	France
202	Gregory XI	30 Dec 1370	27 Mar 1378	7y 2m	France
203	Urban VI	8 Apr 1378	15 Oct 1389	11y 6m	Italy
204	Boniface IX	2 Nov 1389	1 Oct 1404	14y 11m	Italy
205	Innocent VII	17 Oct 1404	6 Nov 1406	2y 19d	Italy
206	Gregory XII	30 Nov 1406	4 July 1415	8y 7m	Italy
207	Martin V	11 Nov 1417	20 Feb 1431	13y 3m	Italy
208	Eugene IV	3 Mar 1431	23 Feb 1447	15y 11m	Italy
209	Nicholas V	6 Mar 1447	24 Mar 1455	8y 18d	Italy
210	Callistus III	8 Apr 1455	6 Aug 1458	3y 4m	Spain
211	Pius II	19 Aug 1458	15 Aug 1464	6y	Italy
212	Paul II	30 Aug 1464	26 July 1471	6y 11m	Italy
213	Sixtus IV	9 Aug 1471	12 Aug 1484	13y	Italy
214	Innocent VIII	29 Aug 1484	25 July 1492	7y 11m	Italy
215	Alexander VI	11 Aug 1492	18 Aug 1503	11y	Spain
216	Pius III	22 Sep 1503	18 Oct 1503	26 days	Italy
217	Julius II	1 Nov 1503	21 Feb 1513	9y 3m	Italy
218	Leo X	11 Mar 1513	1 Dec 1521	8y 8m	Italy
219	Hadrian VI	9 Jan 1522	14 Sep 1523	1y 8m	Netherlands

#	Papal Name	Start of reign	End of reign	Length	From
220	Clement VII	19 Nov 1523	25 Sep 1534	10y 10m	Italy
221	Paul III	13 Oct 1534	10 Nov 1549	15y 1m	Italy
222	Julius III	8 Feb 1550	23 Mar 1555	5y 1m	Italy
223	Marcellus II	9 Apr 1555	1 May 1555	22 days	Italy
224	Paul IV	23 May 1555	18 Aug 1559	4y 2m	Italy
225	Pius IV	25 Dec 1559	9 Dec 1565	5y 11m	Italy
226	St. Pius V	7 Jan 1566	1 May 1572	6y 3m	Italy
227	Gregory XIII	14 May 1572	10 Apr 1585	12y 11m	Italy
228	Sixtus V	24 Apr 1585	27 Aug 1590	5y 4m	Italy
229	Urban VII	15 Sep 1590	27 Sep 1590	12 days	Italy
230	Gregory XIV	5 Dec 1590	16 Oct 1591	10m	Italy
231	Innocent IX	29 Oct 1591	30 Dec 1591	62 days	Italy
232	Clement VIII	30 Jan 1592	5 Mar 1605	13y 1m	Italy
233	Leo XI	1 Apr 1605	27 Apr 1605	26 days	Italy
234	Paul V	16 May 1605	28 Jan 1621	15y 8m	Italy
235	Gregory XV	9 Feb 1621	8 July 1623	2y 4m	Italy
236	Urban VIII	6 Aug 1623	29 July 1644	20y 11m	Italy
237	Innocent X	15 Sep 1644	1 Jan 1655	10y 3m	Italy
238	Alexander VII	7 Apr 1655	22 May 1667	12y 1m	Italy
239	Clement IX	20 June 1667	9 Dec 1669	2y 5m	Italy
240	Clement X	29 Apr 1670	22 July 1676	6y 2m	Italy
241	Innocent XI	21 Sep 1676	12 Aug 1689	12y 10m	Italy
242	Alexander VIII	6 Oct 1689	1 Feb 1691	1y 3m	Italy
243	Innocent XII	12 July 1691	27 Sep 1700	9y 2m	Italy
244	Clement XI	23 Nov 1700	19 Mar 1721	20y 4m	Italy
245	Innocent XIII	8 May 1721	7 Mar 1724	2y 10m	Italy
246	Benedict XIII	29 May 1724	21 Feb 1730	5y 8m	Italy
247	Clement XII	12 July 1730	6 Feb 1740	9y 6m	Italy
248	Benedict XIV	17 Aug 1740	3 May 1758	17y 8m	Italy
249	Clement XIII	16 July 1758	2 Feb 1769	10y 6m	Italy
250	Clement XIV	19 May 1769	22 Sep 1774	5y 4m	Italy
251	Pius VI	15 Feb 1775	29 Aug 1799	24y 6m	Italy
252	Pius VII	14 Mar 1800	20 Aug 1823	23y 5m	Italy

#	Papal Name	Start of reign	End of reign	Length	From
253	Leo XII	28 Sep 1823	10 Feb 1829	5y 4m	Italy
254	Pius VIII	31 Mar 1829	30 Nov 1830	1y 8m	Italy
255	Gregory XVI	2 Feb 1831	1 June 1846	15y 4m	Italy
256	Pius IX	16 June 1846	7 Feb 1878	31y 7m	Italy
257	Leo XIII	20 Feb 1878	20 July 1903	25y 5m	Italy
258	St. Pius X	4 Aug 1903	20 Aug 1914	11y 16d	Italy
259	Benedict XV	3 Sep 1914	22 Jan 1922	7y 4m	Italy
260	Pius XI	6 Feb 1922	10 Feb 1939	17y 4d	Italy
261	Pius XII	2 Mar 1939	9 Oct 1958	19y 7m	Italy
262	John XXIII	28 Oct 1958	3 June 1963	4y 7m	Italy
263	Paul VI	21 June 1963	6 Aug 1978	15y 1m	Italy
264	John Paul I	26 Aug 1978	28 Sep 1978	33 days	Italy
265	John Paul II	16 Oct 1978	2 Apr 2005	26y 5m	Poland
266	Benedict XVI	19 Apr 2005			Germany

APPENDIX C:
THE NAMES
AT A GLANCE

THE 81 ELEMENTAL NAMES

Shown here in alphabetical order. In the case of the 36 repeated names, the two numbers shown within parenthesis denote the number of times that the name was used and the number of times it was assumed. A corresponding list on page 70 shows these 81 elemental names in the order in which they occurred – along with an indication of their span.

Adeodatus; Agapetus (2, 0); Agatho; Alexander (7, 6); Anacletus; Anastasius (4, 1); Anicetus; Anterus; Benedict *[IX just once]* (15, 8); Boniface (8, 2); Caius; Callistus (3, 2); Celestine (5, 4); Clement (14, 13); Conon; Constantine; Cornelius; Damasus (2, 1); Deusdedit; Dionysius; Donus; Eleutherius; Eugene (4, 2); Eusebius; Eutychian; Evaristus; Fabian; Felix (3, 0); Formosus; Gelasius (2, 1); Gregory (16, 12); Hadrian (6, 2); Hilarius; Honorius (4, 3); Hormisdas; Hyginus; Innocent (13, 12); John (21, 8); John Paul (2, 2); Julius (3, 1); Lando; Leo (13, 5); Liberius; Linus; Lucius (3, 2); Marcellinus; Marcellus (2, 0); Marinus (2, 0); Mark; Martin (3, 2); Miltiades; Nicholas (5, 4); Paschal (2, 1); Paul (6, 5); Pelagius (2, 0); Peter; Pius (12, 11); Pontian; Romanus; Sabinian; Sergius (4, 1); Severinus; Silverius; Silvester (3, 2); Simplicius; Siricius; Sisinnius; Sixtus (5, 2); Soter; Stephen (10, 1); Symmachus; Telesphorus; Theodore (2, 0); Urban (8, 2); Valentine; Victor (3, 2); Vigilius; Vitalian; Zacharias; Zephyrinus and Zosimus.

THE 45 NAMES THAT OCCURRED JUST ONCE

In order of occurrence with the sequence numbers in parenthesis:

1. Peter (#1)	2. Linus (#2)	3. Anacletus (#3)
4. Evaristus (#5)	5. Telesphorus (#8)	6. Hyginus (#9)
7. Anicetus (#11)	8. Soter (#12)	9. Eleutherius (#13)
10. Zephyrinus (#15)	11. Pontain (#18)	12. Anterus (#19)
13. Fabian (#20)	14. Cornelius (#21)	15. Dionysius (#25)
16. Eutychian (#27)	17. Caius (#28)	18. Marcellinus (#29)

19. Eusebiusor (#31)   20. Miltiades (#32)   21. Marcus (#34)

22. Liberius (#36)   23. Siricius (#38)   24. Zosimus (#41)

25. Hilarius (#46)   26. Simplicius (#47)   27. Symmachus (#51)

28. Hormisdas (#52)   29. Silverius (#58)   30. Vigilius (#59)

31. Sabinian (#65)   32. Deusdedit (#68)   33. Severinus (#71)

34. Vitalian (#76)   35. Adeodatus (#77)   36. Donus (#78)

37. Agatho (#79)   38. Conon (#83)   39. Sisinnius (#87)

40. Constantine (#88)   41. Zachary (#91)   42. Valentine (#101)

43. Formosus (#112)   44. Romanus (#115)   45. Lando (#122)

In alphabetical order they are:

Adeodatus (#77); Agatho (#79); Anacletus (#3); Anicetus (#11); Anterus (#19); Caius (#28); Conon (#83); Constantine (#88); Cornelius (#21); Deusdedit (#68); Dionysius (#25); Donus (#78); Eleutherius (#13); Eusebiusor (#31); Eutychian (#27); Evaristus (#5); Fabian (#20); Formosus (#112); Hilarius (#46); Hormisdas (#52); Hyginus (#9); Lando (#122); Liberius (#36); Linus (#2); Marcellinus (#29); Marcus (#34); Miltiades (#32); Peter (#1); Pontain (#18); Romanus (#115); Sabinian (#65); Severinus (#71); Silverius (#58); Simplicius (#47); Siricius (#38); Sisinnius (#87); Soter (#12); Symmachus (#51); Telesphorus (#8); Valentine (#101); Vigilius (#59); Vitalian (#76); Zachary (#91); Zephyrinus (#15) and Zosimus (#41).

THE 36 REPEATED NAMES

In order of *first* occurrence with the sequence number of that occurrence in parenthesis:

1. Clement (#4)   2. Alexander (#6)   3. Sixtus (#7)

4. Pius (#10)   5. Victor (#14)   6. Callistus (#16)

7. Urban (#17)   8. Lucius (#22)   9. Stephen (#23)

10. Felix (#26)   11. Marcellus (#30)   12. Silvester (#33)

13. Julius (#35)   14. Damasus (#37)   15. Anastasius (#39)

16. Innocent (#40)   17. Boniface (#42)   18. Celestine (#43)

19. Leo (#45)   20. Gelasius (#49)   21. John (#53)

22. Agapetus (#57)   23. Pelagius (#60)   24. Benedict (#62)

25. Gregory (#64)	26. Honorius (#70)	27. Theodore (#73)
28. Martin (#74)	29. Eugene (#75)	30. Sergius (#84)
31. Paul (#94)	32. Hadrian (#96)	33. Paschal (#99)
34. Nicholas (#106)	35. Marinus (#109)	36. John Paul (#264)

In alphabetical order they, along with the total number of times they occurred shown within parenthesis, are:

Agapetus (2); Alexander (7); Anastasius (4); Benedict (15); Boniface (8); Callistus (3); Celestine (5); Clement (14); Damasus (2); Eugene (4); Felix (3); Gelasius (2); Gregory (16); Hadrian (6); Honorius (4); Innocent (13); John (21); John Paul (2); Julius (3); Leo (13); Lucius (3); Marcellus (2); Marinus (2); Martin (3); Nicholas (5); Paschal (2); Paul (6); Pelagius (2); Pius (12); Sergius (4); Silvester (3); Sixtus (5); Stephen (10); Theodore (2); Urban (8) and Victor (3).

A BREAKDOWN OF THE 36 REPEATED NAMES

In descending order of prevalence. Underlined <u>ordinals</u> denote name was assumed. Consecutive usage is indicated by shading. Additional statistics included for the top tend names.

	TIMES USED	NAME [# times assumed]	ORDINALS OF THE POPES OF THAT NAME AND THEIR SEQUENCE NUMBER
1.	21	John [8] Av. length: 5.81 years Saints: 1	I (53), II (56), III (61), IV (72), V (82), VI (85), VII (86), VIII (108), IX (117), X (123), XI (126), XII (131), XIII (134), XIV (137), XV (138), XVII (141), XVIII (142), XIX (145), XXI (188), XXII (197), XXIII (262)
2.	16	Gregory [12] Av. length: 8.65 years Saints: 4	I (64), II (89), III (90), IV (102), V (139), VI (149), VII (158), VIII (174), IX (179), X (185), XI (202), XII (206), XIII (227), XIV (230), XV (235), XVI (255)
3.	15	Benedict [8] Av. length: 5.27 years Saints: 1	I (62), II (81), III (105), IV (118), V (133), VI (135), VII (136), VIII (144), IX (146, 148 & 151), XI (195), XII (198), XIII (246), XIV (248), XV (259), XVI (266)

| 4. | 14 | Clement [13] Av. length: 8.17 years Saints: 1 | I (4), II (150), III (175), IV (184), V (196), VI (199), VII (220), VIII (232), IX (239), X (240), XI (244), XII (247), XIII (249), XIV (250) |

| 5. | | Innocent [12] Av. length: 8.78 years Saints: 1 | I (40), II (165), III (177), IV (181), V (186), VI (200), VII (205), VIII (214), IX (231), X (237), XI (241), XII (243), XIII (245) |

| 6. | 13 | Leo [5] Av. length: 7.74 years Saints: 5 | I (45), II (80), III (97), IV (104), V (119), VI (124), VII (127), VIII (132), IX (153), X (218), XI (233), XII (253), XIII (257) |

| 7. | 12 | Pius [11] Av. length: 13.53 years Saints: 3 | I (10), II (211), III (216), IV (225), V (226), VI (251), VII (252), VIII (254), IX (256), X (258), XI (260), XII (261) |

| 8. | 10 | Stephen [1] Av. length: 2.56 years Saints: 1 | I (23), II (92), III (93), IV (95), V (98), VI (111), VII (114), VIII (125), IX (128), X (155) |

| 9. | | Boniface [2] Av. length: 5.33 years Saints: 2 | I (42), II (55), III (66), IV (67), V (69), VI (113), VIII (194), IX (204) |

| 10. | 8 | Urban [7] Av. length: 8.22 years Saints: 1 | I (17), II (160), III (173), IV (183), V (201), VI (203), VII (229), VIII (236) |

11.	7	Alexander [6]	I (6), II (157), III (171), IV (182), VI (215), VII (238), VIII (242)
12.	6	Adrian [2]	I (96), II (107), III (110), IV (170), V (187), VI (219)
13.		Paul [5]	I (94), II (212), III (221), IV (224), V (234), VI (263)
14.		Celestine [4]	I (43), II (166), III (176), IV (180), V (193)
15.	5	Nicholas [4]	I (106), II (156), III (189), IV (192), V (209)
16.		Sixtus [2]	I (7), II (24), III (44), IV (213), V (228)
17.		Anastasius [1]	I (39), II (50), III (121), IV (169)
18.	4	Eugene [2]	I (75), II (100), III (168), IV (208)
19.		Honorius [3]	I (70), II (164), III (178), IV (191)
20.		Sergius [1]	I (84), II (103), III (120), IV (143)
21.		Callistus [2]	I (16), II (163), III (210)
22.		Felix [0]	I (26), III (48), IV (54)
23.		Julius [2]	I (35), II (217), III (222)
24.	3	Lucius [2]	I (22), II (167), III (172)
25.		Martin [2]	I (74), IV (190), V (207)
26.		Sylvester [2]	I (33), II (140), III (147)
27.		Victor [2]	I (14), II (154), III (159)
28.		Agapetus [0]	I (57), II (130)
29.		Damasus [1]	I (37), II (152)
30.		Gelasius [1]	I (49), II (162)
31.		John Paul [2]	I (264), II (265)
32.	2	Marcellus [0]	I (30), II (223)
33.		Marinus [0]	I (109), II (129)
34.		Paschal [1]	I (99), II (161)
35.		Pelagius [0]	I (60), II (63)
36.		Theodore [0]	I (73), II (116)

PAINTING & PHOTOGRAPH CREDITS

Figure 1: With permission from (and thanks to) Gloria C. Molinari, the Webmaster for the 'John Paul I' Web site at www.papaluciani.com.

Figures 4 & 15: Copyright expired, public domain photographs from Wikimedia Commons at commons.wikimedia.org.

Figures 5, 6, 8, 16, 18, 20 & 24: From Wikimedia Commons (above) with permission for distribution granted by the copyright holder.

Paintings depicted in the other figures and the front cover:
Copyright expired, public domain images from Wikimedia Commons (above) covered by the 1999 *Bridgeman Art Library v. Corel Corp.* ruling.

All material from Wikimedia Commons (above) used subject to all of their caveats with nothing added or subtracted. Please refer to Wikimedia Commons if you wish to use any of these images.

FRONT COVER: *'Christ handing the keys to kingdom of heaven to St. Peter'*, a fresco painted 1481-1483 on the walls of the Sistine Chapel [p. 89] by Pietro Perugino (1448-1523).

SELECT REFERENCES

📖 Kelly, J. N. D., *The Oxford Dictionary of Popes*, Oxford University Press, 2005.

📖 Maxwell-Stuart, P. G., *Chronicle of the Popes*, Thames and Hudson, 1997.

📖 Duffey, Eamon, *Saints & Sinners: History of the Popes*, Yale University Press, 2001.

📖 Elliott, Lawrence, *I will be called John*, Reader's Digest Press, 1973

📖 Baumgartner, Frederic J., *A History of the Papal Elections*, Palgrave Macmillan, 2003.

⌨ Wikipedia at www.wikipedia.org.

⌨ The Catholic Encyclopedia at www.newadvent.org.

⌨ The Vatican Web site at www.vatican.va.

⌨ www.thinkbabynames.com.

⌨ www.behindthename.com.

⌨ www.20000-names.com.

PARTIAL INDEX

This is not meant to be an exhaustive index. Given that this book is all about names, trying to index each mention of a name would result in a very long, unwieldy index. So, this is but a token index. For a start, most of the prior names are not listed. Please use Appendix A to correlate papal names with prior names, and then refer to the papal name in this index. Names appearing in lists or tables are also not indexed. Readers are urged to peruse the lists and tables since they may contain unexpected information.

Agapetus, 109
Alexander, 80, 109
Alexander II, 105-106
Alexander III, 92, 95, 98, 105, 107
Alexander IV, 101, 107
Alexander VI, 92, 95, 106
Alexander VII, 92, 95-96, 98
Alexander VIII, 96, 101
Ambrose, St., 91, 108
Anacletus, 25, 34, 37, 43, 109
Anastasius, 69
Anastasius I, 17, 40, 54
Anastasius II, 40, 54
Anastasius III, 101
Anastasius IV, 101
Anicetus, 38
Anterus, 2, 40
Arian Controversy, 46
Augustine, St., 19, 108
Avignon, 60-61, 67, 104, 107, 109

Benedict, 57, 73, 76-79, 81, 91-93, 96
Benedict VI, 26, 42
Benedict VII, 8, 42
Benedict VIII, 58, 98, 105
Benedict IX, 11, 58, 98, 102, 106
Benedict XI, 79,98-100
Benedict XII, 67, 108
Benedict XIII, 99, 110
Benedict (XIII), antipope, 60-61
Benedict XIV, 101, 108
Benedict XV, 96-97, 102-103, 108
Benedict XVI, 5, 15, 22, 80-81, 92-93, 96, 102, 108, 110
Benedict, eggs, 110
Benedict of Nursia, St., 97, 108
Benedictine, 11

Bishop of Rome, 6, 16-19, 23-24, 26, 74, 109; first sole, 16, 74
Boniface, 40, 53-55, 57, 78, 81, 96, 100, 104
Boniface I, 53-54
Boniface II, 28, 55
Boniface III, 55
Boniface IV, 55
Boniface V, 100, 104
Boniface VIII, 12, 98, 100, 104
Boniface IX, 12, 60-61, 79, 100, 104
Boniface, antipope, 26, 33, 83
Bull, 21

Cadaver Synod, 10, 69
Callistus, 77, 92-93
Callistus II, 104, 106
Callistus III, 104-105
Cardinals, 1, 5, 11, 14, 30, 60-62, 73, 82, 91, 93-96, 100-101, 103-104, 108
Catelinus, 8, 26, 40, 43-44, 56, 102
Celestine, 78-79
Celestine I, 87, 108
Celestine II, 108
Celestine III, 100-101
Celestine IV, 100, 107
Celestine V, 11-12, 107
Cistercian, 108
Clement, 4, 47-52, 57, 73, 78-79, 93, 100
Clement I, 98, 106
Clement II, 106
Clement III, 106-107
Clement IV, 104, 106-107
Clement V, 104, 107
Clement VI, 12, 107
Clement VII, 30, 98
Clement VIII, 98, 100

Clement (VII), antipope, 60
Clement IX, 99, 106
Clement X, 81, 101
Clement XI, 50-51, 98, 103
Clement XII, 101
Clement XIII, 101
Clement XIV, 101
Cletus, 25, 34, 43, 109
Conon, 109
Constantine, 73
Constantine, Emperor, 46, 73
Constantinople, 8, 26, 33, 56, 108
Cornelius, 40
Cosa, Baldassare, 61-62, 82-84
Crescentii, family, 26-27, 32-33, 105

Damasus I, 17, 59, 69, 76
Damasus II, 106
Decretals, 17
Dionysis, 2
Dominican, 12, 92, 99
Donus, 109
Duo sunt (two power), 58, 99, 104

Eleutherius, 23
Eugene, 73
Eugene I, 100, 108
Eugene III, 79, 100, 108
Eugene IV, 10, 100, 108
Eusebius, 59
Eutychian, 93
Evaristus, 37, 43

Fabian, 39-40, 44
Felix, 40, 54, 79, 109
Felix (II), antipope, 46
Formosus, 10, 93, 102, 109
Franciscans, 89-90, 99

Gelasius I, 19, 58, 69, 76, 93, 99, 104
Gelasius II, 58, 69, 76, 99, 104
Giovanni, 31, 57
Giuliano, 31
Great Western Schism, 60, 105
Greek, 34, 37-39, 41, 53, 86
Greogrian calendar, 110
Gregorian chant, 110
Gregory, 47-48, 50-52, 57-58, 73, 76-78, 93, 102
Gregory I, 19, 28, 58, 94-95, 98, 102, 108, 110
Gregory II, 42, 108
Gregory III, 42

Gregory V, 28-29, 31-32, 45, 84, 98, 102
Gregory VI, 58, 102-103
Gregory VII, 17, 78, 102, 107
Gregory VIII, 108
Gregory IX, 101, 107
Gregory X, 11, 59, 79, 107
Gregory XI, 60, 106-107
Gregory XII, 60-61, 108
Gregory XIII, 91, 98, 102, 110
Gregory XIV, 101
Gregory XV, 94, 98
Gregory XVI, 15, 94-95, 99-100, 107, 110

Hadrian I, 12, 99, 108
Hadrian III, 79
Hadrian IV, 108
Hadrian V, 99
Hadrian VI, 6, 29-31, 45
Hebrew, 41
Honorius I, 101
Honorius II, 101, 107
Honorius III, 101, 107
Honorius IV, 101
Honorius, Emperor, 53
Hormisdas, 55, 79

Innocent, 47-52, 57, 73, 78-79, 92-93
Innocent I, 17, 53, 102
Innocent II, 101, 103, 108
Innocent III, 101-102
Innocent IV, 102, 104
Innocent V, 11-12, 79, 104, 108
Innocent VI, 104
Innocent VII, 60, 105, 108
Innocent VIII, 105, 107
Innocent IX, 108
Innocent X, 107
Innocent XI, 51, 79, 101
Innocent XII, 51, 101
Innocent XIII, 51, 101
Interregnums, 80, 104
Irenaeus, St., 23

Jerome, St., 17
Joan, 82
John, 4, 31-32, 40, 44, 45, 48, 52, 54-55, 57, 60-62, 73, 75-85, 93, 96, 102, 104-105
John: numbering discrepancy, 82; popularity, 57; undocumented ('phantom'), 82-85
John I, 2-3, 8-9, 56, 102
John II, 2-4, 8, 25-26, 44, 79, 97, 102
John III, 8, 26, 43, 102
John IV, 56, 103

John V, 56
John VI, 42, 56
John VII, 42, 57
John XI 9, 101-102
John XII, 8, 26, 57-58, 101-103
John XIII, 32, 45
John XIV, 8, 26-27, 32-33, 45, 82-84, 102
John XV, 27-28, 32-33, 69, 82-84
John XVI, 32
John XVII, 32, 48
John XVIII, 11, 32-33, 48, 57, 84
John XIX, 58-59, 75, 84, 104-105
John XXI, 59-60, 75, 84, 92, 104
John XXII, 60-61, 75, 104
John XXIII/(XXIII), 48, 52, 61-62, 75, 79, 81-82, 92, 96-98, 101-102
John Paul, 4, 42, 47-48, 50, 52, 68-69, 73, 76, 80, 93, 102
John Paul I, 1-3, 100-101
John Paul II, 3, 13, 15, 22, 30, 52, 92-93, 101
John, the Apostle, 8, 102
John, the Baptist, 8, 102
Julius, 69, 93
Julius II, 6, 24, 31, 34, 45, 86, 89, 99
Julius III, 30, 99, 106
Justin: I & II, Emperors, 9

Lando, 68, 109
Lateran Bascilica, 26, 53, 97
Lateran Treaty, 20
Latin, 34-35, 37, 40, 41
Leo, 52, 57, 77-78, 93, 109
Leo I, 102, 106
Leo V, 9
Leo IX, 78, 106
Leo X, 29, 101, 106
Leo XI, 101
Leo XII, 102-103
Leo XIII, 12-13, 78, 103
Liber Pontificalis, 17, 35, 85
Liberius, 46
Linus, 38, 106, 109
Luciani, Albino, 1-2
Lucius, 40
Lucius II, 106, 108
Lucius III, 108

Malachy, St., 5, 11
Marcellinus, 2, 80
Marcellus, 1-3, 76-77, 80
Marcellus II, 6, 30, 45, 91
Marcus, 93

Marinus I, 104
Marinus II, 104
Mark, 2, 40
Martin I, 104
Martin I, 98
Martin II, 104
Martin IV, 73
Martin V, 98
Martin, 103-104
Martin, 73
Matthew, 73, 93
Medici, 29-30, 89, 98
Mercurius, 2-3, 8, 25-26, 40, 44, 56, 102
Michelangelo, 23, 31, 50
Miltiades, 93
Monoepiscopal, 16

Name change, history, 5, 29, 34, 47
Name: original, 14; popularity, 4-5, 47, 77
Names: assumed, 4,35, 68-70, 73; biblical, 73; birth, 68; durability, 76; first documented change, 4; future, 91; innovation, 1; longest unbroken run, 4, 34; most prevalent prior name, 4; multiple use, 4, 68; never assumed, 68; new, 1; popularity, 77; rationale for selection, 94-109; recurrence, 75; repeated, 68; rules, 1; secular use, 110; significant facts, 4, 68; successive, 42; taxonomy, 68; total numbers, 4, 68; used just once, 68
Nicholas, 93
Nicholas I, 102
Nicholas III, 99
Nicholas IV, 11, 101
Nicholas V, 73, 99

Octavian, 8, 26, 45, 57
Otto II, Emperor, 8, 26-27
Otto III, Emperor, 27-28, 32

Paddy Power, 5, 91
Papal Names: 53; history, 23-45; trends, 47-67
Papal Primacy, 19, 93, 102, 106
Papal Titles, 16
Paschal, 69
Paschal I, 108
Paschal II, 108
Paul, 49, 52, 73, 93
Paul, the Apostle, 13-14, 22, 34, 38, 42, 103
Paul I, 103
Paul II, 10, 102-103, 108
Paul III, 30, 98, 108

Paul IV, 59, 90
Paul V, 98, 100
Paul VI, 101, 103
Paul IX, 101
Pelagius, 43, 76, 93
Peter: avoid reusing, 6-8; the list, 10
Peter, St., 5-13, 16-18, 22-24, 34, 36, 42-43, 68, 93, 106
Peter's Years, 12
Pienza, 75
Pisa, 61
Pius, 48-52, 57, 73, 75, 77, 80-81, 92-93, 100, 109
Pius I, 16
Pius II, 74-75, 94, 100-101
Pius III, 94, 100-101
Pius IV, 90, 100, 103
Pius IX, 13, 49, 79-80, 100-101, 103
Pius V, 49-50, 78, 91-92, 103
Pius VI, 49-50, 80, 94-95, 103
Pius VII, 50, 80, 95, 100-101
Pius VIII, 49, 95, 100-101
Pius X, 49, 78, 103
Pius XI, 20, 62, 101, 103
Pius XII, 52, 62, 80, 101
Pontian, 11
Pope: first use, 16; official titles, 18-21; phantom, 33, 82-85; signature, 21
Popes: beatification, 78; canonization, 78; length of reigns, 78-81
Presbyters, 16, 53

Ratzinger, Joseph, 5, 92, 96-97
Regnal Name, 15, 109
Roncalli, Angelo Giuseppe, 62, 96

Sergius, 69, 75
Sergius I, 9, 33, 105
Sergius II, 9
Sergius III, 9
Sergius IV, 9, 33-34, 105
Silverius, 11
Silvester I, 99
Silvester II, 99, 106
Silvester III, 58, 99, 106
Simon, 6, 73

Siricius, 16-17, 19
Sistine Chapel, 5, 23, 31, 50, 85, 89-90, 101, 105, 110
Sixtus/Xystus, 4, 23-24, 34-37, 43, 46, 51, 54-55, 79, 85-91, 93
Sixtus I, 23, 25, 34, 37, 39-40, 43, 54, 85-86
Sixtus II, 23, 51, 54, 86, 98
Sixtus III, 23, 46, 87-88, 91
Sixtus IV, 23, 89-90, 98-99
Sixtus V, 90, 99, 107
Stephen, 42, 47, 57, 69, 78, 81, 96
Stephen I, 69, 98
Stephen II, 80
Stephen IX, 69, 98
Stephen VI, 10, 69

Tusculan, 58-59, 104-105

Urban, 77-78, 93
Urban II, 79, 98, 106-107
Urban III, 100, 107
Urban IV, 98, 100, 109
Urban V, 79, 109
Urban VI, 60, 101, 109
Urban VII, 109
Urban VIII, 22, 73, 109

Vatican Council: First, 13, 20; Second, 20, 22, 103
Victor, 38, 93, 109
Victor I, 93
Victor II, 105-106
Victor III, 79, 105
Vigilius, 93

Wojtyla, Karol Józef, 101

Xystus/Sixtus 23-24, 34-37, 43, 46, 51, 54-55, 79, 85-91, 93

Zacharias, 93
Zephryrinus, 2, 38-40, 44
Zosimus, 53-54, 87

666, 24, 88

FOR YOUR NOTES:

Web site for this book: www.popes-and-papacy.com

ABOUT THE AUTHOR

Anura Guruge was born in Ceylon, came of age in Britain (an Anglophile to the core), and has lived in the U.S. since 1985.

For over 30 years he tried to make a living in the computer industry and was employed by the likes of IBM, Wang and BBN. Due to a genetic disposition, writing, however, is his weakness. He wrote his first book in 1983, 500 pages in longhand, in pencil, distrusting early PCs and too inept to use a typewriter. It was about a networking architecture, now long obsolete. The book, nonetheless, is still sold on the Internet. Since then, he has written four other dense books on technology and upwards of 350 published articles.

Sometimes when the planets are propitiously aligned, he produces graphic marketing collateral for select clients and creates image-laden Web sites.

His first name means 'a guiding light,' while 'Guruge' stands for 'from the house of the teacher.' Both his parents were teachers. But he is not sure whether he has ever lived up to his name.

His mother, and since then quite a few others, refer to him as 'Anu.' In his 30s, he discovered that Babylonians paid homage to an 'Anu.' His mother is unlikely to have known that. He has never had any desire to change any of his names.

He holds a master's degree in Computer Science from the University of London and a bachelor's degree in Computer Technology from the University of Wales. Having once lived in the original Hampshire, he now lives in New Hampshire.

Web site: www.guruge.com

Web site for this book: www.popes-and-papacy.com

Printed in the United States
117900LV00002B/292-300/P